UNIVERSITY OF
WINC...

Digital Education and Learning

Series Editors
Michael Thomas
University of Central Lancashire
Preston, United Kingdom

John Palfrey
Phillips Academy
Andover, Massachusetts, USA

Mark Warschauer
University of California
Irvine, California, USA

Much has been written during the first decade of the new millennium about the potential of digital technologies to produce a transformation of education. Digital technologies are portrayed as tools that will enhance learner collaboration and motivation and develop new multimodal literacy skills. Accompanying this has been the move from understanding literacy on the cognitive level to an appreciation of the sociocultural forces shaping learner development. Responding to these claims, the Digital Education and Learning Series explores the pedagogical potential and realities of digital technologies in a wide range of disciplinary contexts across the educational spectrum both in and outside of class. Focusing on local and global perspectives, the series responds to the shifting landscape of education, the way digital technologies are being used in different educational and cultural contexts, and examines the differences that lie behind the generalizations of the digital age. Incorporating cutting edge volumes with theoretical perspectives and case studies (single authored and edited collections), the series provides an accessible and valuable resource for academic researchers, teacher trainers, administrators and students interested in interdisciplinary studies of education and new and emerging technologies.

More information about this series at
http://www.springer.com/series/14952

Michael Flavin

Disruptive Technology Enhanced Learning

The Use and Misuse of Digital Technologies in Higher Education

palgrave
macmillan

Michael Flavin
King's College London
London, United Kingdom

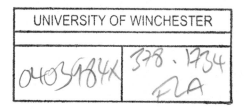

Digital Education and Learning
ISBN 978-1-137-57283-7   ISBN 978-1-137-57284-4   (eBook)
DOI 10.1057/978-1-137-57284-4

Library of Congress Control Number: 2017930493

This Palgrave Macmillan imprint is published by Springer Nature
The registered company is Macmillan Publishers Ltd.
The registered company address is: The Campus, 4 Crinan Street, London, N1 9XW, United Kingdom

To Geraldine, Liam and Rosie

SERIES PREFACE

Much has been written during the start of this millennium about the potential of digital technologies to radically transform education and learning. Typically, such calls for change spring from the argument that traditional education no longer engages learners or teaches them the skills required for the twenty-first century. Digital technologies are often described as tools that will enhance collaboration and motivate learners to re-engage with education and enable them to develop the new multimodal literacy skills required for today's knowledge economy. Using digital technologies is a creative experience in which learners actively engage with solving problems in authentic environments that underline their productive skills rather than merely passively consuming knowledge. Accompanying this argument has been the move from understanding literacy on the cognitive level to an appreciation of the sociocultural forces shaping learner development and the role communities play in supporting the acquisition of knowledge.

Emerging from this context the Digital Education and Learning series was founded to explore the pedagogical potential and realities of digital technologies in a wide range of disciplinary contexts across the educational spectrum around the world. Focusing on local and global perspectives, this series responds to the shifting demands and expectations of educational stakeholders, explores the ways new technologies are actually being used in different educational and cultural contexts, and examines the opportunities

and challenges that lie behind the myths and rhetoric of digital age education. This series encourages the development of evidence-based research
that is rooted in an understanding of the history of technology, as well as
open to the potential for new innovation, and adopts critical perspectives on
technological determinism as well as techno-scepticism.

While the potential for changing the way we learn in the digital age is
significant, and new sources of information and forms of interaction have
developed, many educational institutions and learning environments have
changed little from those that existed over one hundred years ago. Whether
in the form of smartphones, laptops or tablets, digital technologies may be
increasingly ubiquitous in a person's social life but marginal in their daily
educational experience once they enter a classroom. Although many people
increasingly invest more and more time on their favourite social media site,
integrating these technologies into curricula or formal learning environments remains a significant challenge, if indeed it is a worthwhile aim in the
first place. History tells us that change in educational contexts, if it happens
at all in ways that were intended, is typically more incremental' and rarely
'revolutionary'. Understanding the development of learning technologies
in the context of a historically informed approach therefore is one of the
core aspects of this series, as is the need to understand the increasing
internationalisation of education and the way learning technologies are
culturally mediated. While the digital world appears to be increasingly
'flat', significant challenges continue to exist, and this series will
problematize terms that have sought to erase cultural, pedagogical and
theoretical differences rather than to understand them. 'Digital natives',
'digital literacy', 'digital divide', 'digital media'—these and such mantras as
'twenty-first century learning'—are phrases that are being used in ways that
require further clarification and critical engagement rather than unquestion-
ing and uncritical acceptance.

This series aims to examine the complex discourse of digital technologies
and to understand the implications for teaching, learning and professional
development. By mixing volumes with theoretical perspectives with case
studies detailing actual teaching approaches, whether on or off campus, in
face-to-face, fully online or blended learning contexts, the series will examine the emergence of digital technologies from a range of new international
and interdisciplinary perspectives. Incorporating original and innovative
volumes with theoretical perspectives and case studies (single authored

and edited collections), the series aims to provide an accessible and valuable resource for academic researchers, teacher trainers, administrators, policymakers and learners interested in cutting-edge research on new and emerging technologies in education.

Michael Thomas
John Palfrey
Mark Warschauer

ACKNOWLEDGEMENTS

I am grateful to Dr Stylianos Hatzipanagos for his feedback on an earlier draft of Chap. 2 and to my research assistant, Valentina Quintero-Rodriguez.

CONTENTS

LIST OF FIGURES

CHAPTER 1

Introduction

This introductory chapter sets out the theoretical frameworks used in the book, provides a chapter by chapter summary and introduces the book's core arguments.

Technology has promised a lot to education. The telephone, film and radio were all going to revolutionize the classroom. Television promised to be similarly transformational, as did the internet (Bok 2003; Flavin 2016; Horrigan 2016). Yet, and despite generations of technological onslaught, education systems have not changed fundamentally, and the university as an institution appears remarkably resilient; Gordon (2014) in a Higher Education Academy (HEA) report in the UK states university education 'is likely to remain the gold standard for some time' (p. 21). Technologies come and go but the university remains, in a recognizable and largely unchanged form.

Why has the internet not truly revolutionized learning and teaching in universities? To those who argue that it has, it can be pointed out that the lecture is still the dominant pedagogical tool, and the essay and the exam remain the dominant assessment instruments. This book therefore attempts to address the issue of technology use and misuse in higher education by identifying and analysing disruptive technologies, their impact and universities' responses.

The aim of this book is to understand how universities can engage constructively with disruptive technologies for learning and teaching (when this book uses the word 'technologies' it is referring to digital technologies). It is not the purpose of this book to predict what technologies will be adopted in

© The Author(s) 2017
M. Flavin, *Disruptive Technology Enhanced Learning*,
DOI 10.1057/978-1-137-57284-4_1

the future to support learning and teaching in higher education, though the book does identify criteria and practices that are relevant in this respect. The book pursues its aim by examining how technologies are used in practice to support learning and teaching in higher education. In addition, the book examines the implications of disruptive technology usage. Universities can engage constructively with disruptive technologies by recognizing the ways students and lecturers use technologies to support their learning and teaching. The book further argues that universities need to understand why disruptive technologies are being used in order to inform their strategies around technology enhanced learning.

The book identifies misalignments between the technologies supplied by universities, often at considerable expense, and the disruptive technologies used in practice by students and lecturers. Moreover, the use of disruptive technologies has implications for the division of labour in higher education, for assessment and for the higher education community as a whole. In addition, the use of disruptive technologies challenges the role of the university as gatekeeper to knowledge and signifies the possibility of a more open borders approach.

Specific disruptive technologies considered in this book include the internet search engine Google and the online encyclopaedia Wikipedia. Both are now established. Head and Eisenberg's (2010) research showed 82% of their undergraduate respondents used Wikipedia to support academic work, though an even greater number used Google. Colon-Aguirre and Fleming-May (2012) interviewed −21 undergraduate students, all of whom used Wikipedia for their research, commonly being directed to Wikipedia following an initial search on Google; one of their interviewees stated, 'I feel like it's hard to get a lot of information out of a book unless you want to read the entire book' (p. 395). Colon-Aguirre and Fleming-May (2012) also state that the majority of their respondents acknowledged that library resources were superior to those found via online search engines, which poses the question, why do users prefer to go online? The answer, this book argues, relates to the simplicity, ease of use and convenience of Google, Wikipedia and similar technologies. By looking at how and why Google and Wikipedia have become established in higher education, we get a sense of disruptive technologies, their appeal and their impact.

The book challenges the argument that a wide range of technologies is used to support learning and teaching and argues instead that students and lecturers use a small range of technologies to accomplish a wide range of tasks. Google is used as a hub technology from which a range of resources is accessed; Hillis et al. (2013) argue, 'the internet and Google and the #hashtag now constitute their [undergraduate students'] primary access to information' (p. 6). Students and lecturers are efficient technology users and are interested in getting jobs done, simply and conveniently.

The term technology enhanced learning, which has become a standard phrase in higher education, is used, as stated by Kirkwood and Price (2014), 'to describe the application of information and communication technologies to teaching and learning' (p. 6); Gordon (2014) defines technology enhanced learning as, 'the use of Information Communication and Technology... in its widest sense to support and improve the learning experience' (p. 4), and the Joint Information Systems Committee (JISC 2009) states that the term emphasizes 'how technology adds value to learning' (p. 8). That said, the term is not universal and has been criticised (Bayne 2015). Furthermore, a Higher Education Funding Council for England (HEFCE) report (2009) resisted a definition of technology enhanced learning, 'it is important not to create fixed definitions,' while recognizing, 'innovative developments in technology will only be relevant if the enhancement of learning and teaching is the core purpose' (p. 8). This book, however, takes the view that technology enhanced learning says enough about learning and teaching with technologies to be useful; the Universities and Colleges Information Systems Association (UCISA 2016) definition, 'Any online facility or system that directly supports learning and teaching. This may include a formal VLE, e-assessment or e-portfolio software, or lecture capture system, mobile app or collaborative tool that supports student learning. This includes any system that has been developed in-house, as well as commercial or open source tools,' (p. 1) is used as a working definition for this book, notwithstanding that it prioritizes institutional over disruptive technologies. This book avoids the Web 2.0 label for technologies (O'Reilly 2005), partly in order not to bombard the reader with too many terms, and partly because there is a risk of the term Web 2.0 lapsing into cliché.

This book responds to a need to better understand how technologies are used in practice in order to practise technology enhanced learning more effectively. Given the ubiquity of technology usage in higher education, there is a need to understand more fully the technology practices of students and lecturers, with a view to rethinking approaches to technology enhanced learning. Kirkwood and Price (2014) summarize articles on technology enhanced learning from 2005 to 2010 and conclude, 'many interventions were technology-led' (p. 25) and 'there seemed to be many cases of deterministic expectations that introducing technology would, *by itself,* bring about changes in teaching/learning practices' (p. 26). For this book, practice is primary. An approach to technology enhanced learning based on practice, rather than on the intrinsic qualities of technologies, enables and encourages engagement with disruptive technologies to support learning and teaching.

A hierarchy of theoretical frameworks is used in the book. Disruptive Innovation is used to identify relevant technologies. Having used Disruptive Innovation to identify disruptive technologies (in Christensen's sense, see below), *Disruptive Technology Enhanced Learning* analyses the impact of Disruptive Innovation on higher education, using Activity Theory (Vygotsky 1930; Leontiev 1978, 1981) to explore how Disruptive Innovation reconfigures learning, teaching and assessment and, more widely, social relations in higher education. Moreover, the book uses second generation Activity Theory (Engeström 1987 (rev edn 2015)) as a lens through which to consider the impact of disruptive technologies on higher education. Recent work is used to analyse current applications of Activity Theory and their relevance to technology enhanced learning.

Finally, the Community of Practice theory (Lave and Wenger 1991; Wenger 1998) is used to complement the main frameworks, to identify and illuminate the community under examination, to outline how technology usage can enable progress within a community and to consider how higher education communities can respond to Disruptive Innovation. The Community of Practice theory enables analysis of how Disruptive Innovation impacts on higher education communities as a whole (identifying the community as the locus of innovation), as well as analysing the structural composition of academic communities and the opportunities and threats posed to universities by Disruptive Technology Enhanced Learning. In essence, Disruptive Innovation identifies technologies, Activity Theory analyses and the Community of Practice theory contextualizes.

These three theories are used in the book to help understand how universities can engage constructively with disruptive technologies for learning and teaching. Universities are in a position to devise strategies for technology enhanced learning based on actual practices with technologies, rather than have strategies determined by technology.

This book therefore views learning and teaching as social practices. Consequently, psychological theories of technology adoption are not applicable because this book sees identity as determined historically and socially. A designed intervention in relation to technology enhanced learning can be conducive to change and may catalyse change, but it does not make change happen in a mono-causal sense; when technological change happens within a higher education community of practice, this book argues that it is caused primarily by social factors identified in the second generation activity system such as changes in rules (for example, assessment methods) or the division of labour.

As this introductory statement has presented a number of specific terms and ideas, these are defined synoptically below. Fuller exploration of each of these terms will be provided in Chaps. 2, 3, and 4.

DISRUPTIVE TECHNOLOGIES AND DISRUPTIVE INNOVATION

The term 'disruptive technology' derives from Clayton Christensen's (1997) book, *The Innovator's Dilemma*. The term is used in this book to signify technologies that are not designed to support learning and teaching but are used by students and lecturers, having found a market and a use value. More precisely, disruptive technologies conform to four key criteria identified by Christensen (1997); they are cheaper, simpler, smaller and more convenient than the rival, incumbent technologies they frequently displace as market leaders (p. xv).

The work of Christensen (Kim B. Clark Professor of Business Administration at the Harvard Business School) has been highly influential in business studies; he argues that well-established, well-run businesses can get unseated by technically inferior rivals, by virtue of the latter's affordability, ease of use and convenience. He defines this process as Disruptive Innovation, which enables innovative goods and services to gain footholds in markets, from which they develop technically and eventually become market leaders. Christensen identifies specific disruptive technologies which prompt new forms of practice, adopting a case study approach (including the disk drive industry and Honda motorcycles in the USA) and basing Disruptive Innovation on the core criteria for disruptive technologies.

Christensen (1997) also constructs a dualism between sustaining technologies and disruptive technologies. The former allow us to do something we had already been doing a little bit better than before (for example, a slightly more fuel-efficient car), whereas the latter prompt new forms of practice (for example, the invention of the car itself).

Disruptive Innovation has critics; Christensen's case study approach is problematic because it allows him to retrospectively cherry pick examples that validate the theory, as argued by Lepore (2014) and Danneels (2004, 2006).

Moreover, Christensen's own venture into predicting Disruptive Innovation, the Disruptive Growth Fund, was singularly unsuccessful, though Christensen has downplayed his role in the Fund (see Chap. 2 and the conclusion). However, from the perspective of this book, Christensen's theory comprises an interesting and revealing lens for exploring both the intrinsic qualities of technologies and their use in practice. Christensen et al. (2011) argue, 'What the theory of disruptive innovation suggests is that the business model of many traditional colleges and universities is broken' (p. 10); it is part of this book's purpose to assess that claim.

ACTIVITY THEORY AND EXPANSIVE LEARNING

This book uses Activity Theory and expansive learning as a lens through which to analyse the impact of disruptive technologies on higher education learning and teaching. The former term, Activity Theory, a framework for analysing purposeful human activity, was conceptualized by Leontiev (1978, 1981) following initial work by Vygotsky (1927, 1930). Expansive learning was devised by Engeström (1987, 2001), whose work was informed significantly by Activity Theory which provided the original, triadic representation (see Chap. 3), which Engeström developed by adding additional social elements to the original formulation. Furthermore, while Vygotsky's work had focused on the development of children and their acquisition of language, Engeström focused on adult learning. References to Activity Theory in this book allude to the original theoretical works on human activity and consciousness with particular reference to the argument that subjectivity is historically and socially determined. References to second generation activity theory refer to Engeström's specific framework for understanding purposeful human conduct and its attendant social relations. Engeström argues that the contradictions within an activity system can result in expansive learning, leading to the creation of a new activity system (Engeström 1987, 2001).

Engeström (in common with Activity Theory) uses the term 'subject' to denote a human participant or participants and uses the term 'tool' to refer to real or symbolic artefacts. Consequently, in this book, 'tool' refers to technology, in the sense of an artefact used to accomplish a purpose. Within an activity system, the term 'object' is used to denote purpose. Consequently, in this book, subjects refer to participants, tools refer to technologies accessed via the internet, and object signifies purpose.

COMMUNITY OF PRACTICE

The Community of Practice theory (Lave and Wenger 1991; Wenger 1998) contextualizes the use of disruptive technologies. For example, individuals on the periphery of a community of practice, such as new entrant students, can have a significant impact by introducing a new technology to their peer or study group. The periphery of a learning community can be a prime site for Disruptive Innovation. The Community of Practice theory therefore enables an understanding of how disruptive technologies can impact on higher education communities, moving from the micro level of the individual learning and teaching situation from an Activity Theory perspective to the macro level of the institution and the higher education sector, through the Community of Practice lens.

This book refers to learning and teaching to describe a pedagogical totality. The book does not distinguish between learning and teaching and examine each separately, because, and in order to reinforce the Community of Practice perspective, a range of roles is seen to be contributing to collective, institutional aims.

The hierarchy of the theoretical frameworks for the book is reflected in the book's chronology. Therefore, most attention is given to the work of Christensen and others around Disruptive Innovation, and secondary attention is given to Activity Theory and expansive learning, a perspective which is used to analyse the impact of the technologies identified as a result of the Disruptive Innovation approach. Finally, the Community of Practice theory is used to contextualize the impact of Disruptive Technology Enhanced Learning in higher education.

TECHNOLOGY USE IN HIGHER EDUCATION

It is a truism to state that technologies support learning and teaching in higher education. At the most mundane level, text messages can be used to alert students about room or lecture time changes. However, the use of institutional technologies such as academic journal aggregators (proprietary databases such as Academic Search Complete) is less widespread, and the use of virtual learning environments (VLEs) is often limited relative to VLEs' design features and potential; Gordon (2014) defines the VLE as 'little other than a flexible and accessible library' (p. 10). VLEs have the potential to transform learning and teaching as they can enable any time anywhere peer collaboration through their discussion facilities. However, discussion facilities on VLEs are often underused (Hemmi et al. 2009). Far from changing pedagogical practices, VLEs have reaffirmed traditional, transmissive modes of teaching.

Disruptive Innovation suggests VLEs are sustaining technologies, offering improvements in terms of access (a VLE allows students to access content at any time, not just in a timetabled slot) but not changing the relationships operating in learning and teaching. That said, if VLEs work well as content repositories, there is an argument for using VLEs in precisely this way. In line with Disruptive Innovation, practice creates purpose, and VLEs are often used, in practice, simply to store and access content.

Students may be making limited use of VLEs, but they are enthusiastic users of technology more widely in their lives; Madge et al. (2009) claim over 95% of UK students regularly use social networking sites. However, out of the 213 students sampled in their research on the use of the social networking site Facebook, less than 10% were in favour of Facebook being used as a teaching tool. Similarly, Jones et al. (2010) found that, while over 70% of their sample of students drawn from four universities had a social networking account, they rarely used social media for educational purposes. These results differ from those presented by Selwyn and Gorard (2016) in an Australian context. Their results indicate Facebook is used by students to support their learning but, in general, students seemingly prefer to demarcate their technology usage, an argument also made by Timmis (2012) and reinforced in this book.

VLEs are used widely but their full range of learning and teaching potential is seldom realized. VLEs are ubiquitous, and students and lecturers use the internet extensively to undertake research (Littlejohn et al. 2012; Henderson et al. 2015b). The use of plagiarism detection software and online submission tools is similarly widespread (UCISA 2014, 2016), highlighting the across-the-board institutional adoption of technologies in higher education. Moreover, students are often energetic users of social networking technologies, but do not in general want to use these technologies to support learning and teaching. Design may enable technologies to perform a range of functions but (and as this book argues) practice determines purpose. Technologies are used widely in higher education to support learning and teaching, but not all individual technologies are used widely, and usage of individual technologies is determined by users who, in turn, determine specific and distinctive purposes for specific technologies.

Assumptions can easily be made about students as users of technologies. Prensky (2001) constructed the dualism of digital natives and digital immigrants to define the space between a generation of students who had grown up with digital technologies and prior generations of teachers to whom the technologies were unfamiliar. However, subsequent research has painted a different picture. Jones and Healing (2010), for example, interviewed first-year undergraduate students in England and found that over a third of the interviewees were not confident about using VLEs (p. 349). Other researches have also shown students to be largely passive users of technologies (for example, Margaryan et al. 2011), while Jelfs and Richardson (2013) found no evidence to support the digital natives hypothesis in a survey of more than 4000 distance learners in higher education. Furthermore, in research involving 1658 undergraduates in Australia, Henderson et al. (2015a) found that students' use of technologies was logistical (catching-up on lecture content, for example) rather than participatory (see also, Flavin 2016). Jones (2012) summarizes the research on digital natives and finds that there is no such thing as a generational cohort (p. 30).

One aspect of technology enhanced learning highlighted by Johnson et al. (2016) in the USA is learning analytics, defined by Siemens and Gasevic (2012) as, 'the collection of data and analytics in order to understand and inform teaching and learning' (p. 1). Learning analytics gathers details of students' actions in online environments. Its aims can include the identification of at-risk students and the gathering of data to effect real-time or just-in-time improvements in learning and teaching.

The use of analytics has commercial implications, analysing data in order to target specific markets through advertising campaigns (Burd et al. 2015). There are, however, limits to the value of data drawn from students' interactions with online resources, because, for example, it records visits undertaken to a VLE but not the quality of learning undertaken on the VLE, a problem recognized by Gasevic et al. (2015) and Rienties et al. (2016).

Learning analytics poses further problems relating to privacy and the safety of student data (Johnson et al. 2016, p. 39). Furthermore, and as identified by Ferguson et al. (2014), learning analytics needs the engagement of learners and teachers, and of support staff and administrators. That said, the reformulation of technology enhanced learning, from providing resources or interaction to providing analysis to determine future delivery, is a radical one with implications for programme content and student support. Baer and Campbell (2012) see analytics as both a sustaining and disruptive innovation; a sustaining innovation in the sense that predictive analytics can identify at-risk students, but a disruptive innovation because analytics could be used 'to power adaptive systems that adapt to the learner's needs based on behaviours of the individual as well as of past students' patterns' (p. 62), thus creating more personalized forms of learning. Sharples et al. (2015) build on learning analytics to identify 'adaptive teaching' (p. 5), whereby data about a learner's online practice can be used to personalize learning, and 'stealth assessment' (p. 5), whereby data on learners' usage of online environments enable ongoing monitoring of their progress. However, Sharples et al. (2015) also note: 'Concerns have been raised about collection of vast amounts of data and the ethics of using computers to monitor a person's every action' (p. 5). Setting ethics to one side, there remains a core issue of using learning analytics effectively, but a significant incentive to personalize learning, an outcome with the potential to enhance learning, teaching, assessment, retention and student satisfaction (Flavin 2016).

Bring Your Own Device (BYOD), the use of mobile devices owned by the user to support learning and teaching (a related term to mobile learning, or m-learning), is increasingly commonplace. Smartphones have become progressively more multifunctional to the point at which they can supersede established technologies. UCISA (2014) identified 'notable progress towards the optimisation of services for mobile devices' (p. 10) and the UCISA survey of 2016 shows 60% of Higher Education institutions optimising services for mobile devices, and with an increase in optimising library services; universities are amending their practices to accommodate BYOD. The growth of smartphones and similar technologies is such that, 'the question is no longer whether to allow them in the classroom, but how to most effectively integrate and support them' (Johnson et al. 2016, p. 36). Johnson et al. (2016) also note the spread of BYOD at universities and argue, 'BYOD policies have been shown to reduce overall technology spending' (p. 36), as the cost of the hardware is shifted from the institution to the individual, a process exemplifying the increasing privatization of higher education. In this sense, BYOD is symptomatic of wider trends, as Lawton et al. (2013) note: 'there is, however, a movement away from public funding towards privately supported higher education. Although this shift now coincides with an economic downturn in large parts of the developed world, it predated it and will not be reversed in the likely event of an economic recovery before 2020. The gradual withdrawal of the state from HE funding in developed countries is set to stay' (p. 43). As individually owned technologies supersede institutional technologies, the role of the institution is reconfigured to the point at which students arguably purchase a brand endorsement but supply the apparatus of learning and teaching themselves. This argument overlooks the expertise of the academic community but highlights how technology use is interwoven with, and influenced by, economic and social factors.

There are disadvantages to BYOD, including the cost, which can exclude users from less privileged backgrounds, and the market for mobile devices, in which obsolescence is a frequent occurrence, given the speed with which technologies advance (Yeap et al. 2016). Gikas and Grant (2013) study the use of mobile devices in higher education and demonstrate how ease of use and convenience are central to their adoption (pp. 21–22), thus implying the value of Disruptive Innovation as a means of better understanding BYOD in higher education. Moreover, if the disruptive technology is affordable, the student is not obviously disadvantaged; a JISC report (2011) claimed, 'The low cost of ownership means that some students can afford newer-specification devices than colleges and universities can supply' (p. 7). As costs fall, so does digital exclusion.

On an institutional level, technology enhanced learning is expensive; a HEFCE report of 2011, *Collaborate to Compete,* noted, 'Quality online learning is not a cheap option' (p. 5). Technology enhanced learning represents a significant investment of time and money on the part of universities, but specific questions of cost remain unclear: 'Costing studies for new technologies have given little help to innovators and managers because they have tried to give a definitive and generalised answer to the question of whether they are cost effective. . . it is not feasible to determine a definitive answer' (Laurillard 2007, p. 38). Smith et al. (2013) further note the problem of costs being expressed quantitatively while benefits are recorded qualitatively, a problem noted previously by Cohen and Nachmias (2006). Cohen and Nachmias (2006) also argue that the highest cost is faculty time, unless technology enhanced learning is made less interactive (p. 85), but this leads to a transmissive curriculum which does little to foster understanding. Technology enhanced learning is costly but actual costs in relation to benefits are hard to pin down. Moreover, the effects of technology enhanced learning are hard to identify and quantify (Flavin 2016).

Having outlined the core ideas in this book and having contextualized the issues through a brief survey of technology use in higher education, a summary of the following chapters is now presented.

CHAPTER SUMMARIES

Chapter 2: 'Free, Simple and Easy to Use: Disruptive Technologies, Disruptive Innovation and Technology Enhanced Learning.' This chapter lays out the core theoretical framework for the book. It summarizes the work of Christensen (1997), which first identified the criteria for disruptive technologies, and Christensen and Raynor (2003), which further developed the theory of Disruptive Innovation.

The chapter also summarizes and analyses more recent work by Christensen, together with subsequent critique of Disruptive Innovation, including sources that argue against the validity of Christensen's approach. The chapter demonstrates how the Disruptive Innovation lens can be applied to technology enhanced learning in higher education, as the theory foregrounds practice over the intrinsic qualities of technologies. Moreover, Christensen's approach is useful for identifying specific disruptive technologies.

The chapter uses case studies from Christensen's work and data from more recent research on Disruptive Innovation. The chapter analyses the challenges posed to technology enhanced learning by Disruptive Innovation, which argues implicitly that technology enhanced learning in higher education has been misdirected to date because it has focused more on technologies than on practice with technologies. The chapter as a whole provides a grounding in Disruptive Innovation and identifies specific disruptive technologies in higher education.

Chapter 3: 'Why Can't I Just Google It? What Disruptive Innovation Means for Higher Education.' Having analysed Disruptive Innovation to understand the use of digital technologies to support learning and teaching in higher education and to identify specific disruptive technologies, this chapter analyses the impact of Disruptive Innovation on higher education. Activity Theory is used as the framework for this chapter, enabling exploration of how students and lecturers interact with technologies. The original research on Activity Theory is surveyed (Vygotsky 1930; Leontiev 1978, 1981), which argues that purposeful human activity is mediated by tools (either material or abstract) in an interactive process. Second generation Activity Theory (Engeström 1987) is also analysed and is especially useful because of its inclusion of social as well as material factors in purposeful human activity. More recent Activity Theory studies are used to analyse contemporary usage of technology tools to achieve specific goals.

The chapter argues that Disruptive Innovation, viewed through an Activity Theory lens, impacts most significantly on social relations in higher education, as the widespread use of disruptive technologies challenges the gatekeeper role of the university, with students and lecturers frequently preferring disruptive sources. The chapter also argues that Disruptive Innovation affects learning, teaching, assessment and the division of labour in higher education because students may by-pass module reading lists and technologies made available by their universities and, instead, select resources of their own choosing, a process facilitated through disruptive technologies and exemplifying Disruptive Innovation.

Chapter 4: 'Whatever Happened to the Digital Natives? Disruptive Innovation in the Higher Education Community of Practice.' This chapter uses Lave and Wenger's (1991) and Wenger's (1998) work on the Community of Practice to understand how Disruptive Innovation impacts on higher education communities. The chapter also engages with more recent critique of the Community of Practice in order to offer a nuanced reading of the Community of Practice theory in relation to Disruptive Technology Enhanced Learning in higher education.

New entrants to a university can be adept users of technologies, but universities may not welcome the new technologies and practices users bring with them. Moreover, students and lecturers may not wish to use the technologies they use to support their social lives to support their learning and teaching lives too. The chapter as a whole locates the role and activity of Disruptive Innovation in higher education communities of practice and analyses the impact of Disruptive Innovation on the higher education sector. The chapter also identifies the periphery of a learning community as a significant locus for innovation.

Chapter 5: 'Bidding the Waves Go Back: Engaging with Disruptive Innovation.' The book is interested primarily in practice with technologies rather than in technologies per se. Universities seek to direct technology usage through technology enhanced learning strategies (a number of which will be surveyed in the chapter), but this book argues that practice is primary, and practice is shaped by a range of factors, including many beyond universities' control, such as marketing, constraints effected by assessment-driven higher education systems and rival demands on the time of both students and lecturers. The conclusion therefore argues for the recognition of Disruptive Innovation in higher education and suggests means by which Disruptive Technology Enhanced Learning can be incorporated within institutional approaches to learning, teaching and assessment. These means include technology enhanced learning strategies based on practice rather than on technologies; the rethinking of institutional technologies to see if they can be reconfigured in line with Disruptive Innovation; and the welcoming of innovative practice, using non-institutional technologies to accomplish educational goals.

The chapter takes Massive Open Online Courses (MOOCs) as a case study and argues MOOCs are not disruptive technologies as, in practice, MOOCs are only simple and easy to use for people who have undertaken higher education study previously; the UCISA report of 2014, for example, indicated that MOOCs had, to date, made little impression (2014, p. 3). The chapter argues that MOOCs are more akin to Second Life, a virtual world which failed to change higher education because, the chapter argues, it failed to conform to Christensen's core criteria, though MOOCs may find a market in Continuing Professional Development courses (Laurillard 2016). The chapter argues for Christensen's core criteria as a practical starting point for the design and application of technologies in higher education.

The conclusion also proposes means by which to enhance learning and teaching in higher education by accommodating the use of disruptive technologies, recognizing that students and lecturers often by-pass institutional resources in their construction of knowledge. The conclusion argues that universities will benefit from engaging with disruptive technologies, recognizing that disruptive technology use happens and that an accommodating approach based on known aspects of practice will enable disruptive technologies to contribute to and enhance learning and teaching in higher education.

The book as a whole offers a fresh perspective on technology enhanced learning by using a range of approaches to investigate the uses of technologies to support learning and teaching in higher education. Previous works have used Disruptive Innovation, Activity Theory or the Community of Practice theory separately, but this book is distinctive in using all three theories in an integrated and coherent approach, to illuminate and analyse technology enhanced learning. The conjoining of Disruptive Innovation with Activity Theory and the Community of Practice theory means that disruption is not just observed, but analysed, too. *Disruptive Technology Enhanced Learning* applies a contemporary and relevant lens to technology enhanced learning, offering new insights and new approaches to the application of technologies for learning, teaching and assessment. *Disruptive Technology Enhanced Learning* is a ground-breaking study of how and why technologies succeed or fail in higher education.

This chapter has introduced the book's area of interest and its core arguments, while also offering a chapter by chapter summary. The next chapter explores in more detail the foundational theoretical framework for this book, Disruptive Innovation.

REFERENCES

Baer, L., & Campbell, J. (2012). From metrics to analytics, reporting to action: Analytics' role in changing the learning environment. In D. G. Oblinger (Ed.), *Game changers: Education and information technologies*. Louisville: Educause.

Bayne, S. (2015). What's the matter with "technology enhanced learning"? *Learning, Media and Technology, 40*(1), 5–20.

Bok, D. (2003). *Universities in the marketplace: The commercialization of higher education*. Princeton/Oxford: Princeton University Press.

Burd, E. L., Smith, S. P., & Reisman, S. (2015). Exploring business models for MOOCs in higher education. *Innovative Higher Education, 40*, 37–49.

Christensen, C. M. (1997). *The innovator's dilemma: When new technologies cause great firms to fail*. Boston: Harvard Business School Press.

Christensen, C. M., & Raynor, M. E. (2003). *The innovator's solution: Creating and sustaining successful growth*. Boston: Harvard Business School Press.

Christensen, C.M., Horn, M.B., Caldera, L., & Soares, L. (2011). *Disrupting college: How disruptive innovation can deliver quality and affordability to postsecondary education*. Mountain View: Center for American Progress and Innosight Institute. Retrieved from https://cdn.americanprogress.org/wp-content/uploads/issues/2011/02/pdf/disrupting_college_execsumm.pdf

Cohen, A., & Nachmias, R. (2006). A quantitative cost effectiveness model for web-supported academic instruction. *Internet and Higher Education, 9*, 81–90.

Colon-Aguirre, M., & Fleming-May, R. A. (2012). "You just type in what you are looking for": Undergraduates' use of library resources vs. Wikipedia. *The Journal of Academic Librarianship, 38*(6), 391–399.

Danneels, E. (2004). Disruptive technology reconsidered: A critique and research agenda. *The Journal of Product Information Management, 21*, 246–258.

Danneels, E. (2006). From the guest editor: Dialogue on the effects of disruptive technology on firms and industries. *The Journal of Product Information Management, 23*, 2–4.

Engeström, Y. (1987). *Learning by expanding: An activity-theoretical approach to developmental research*. Helsinki: Orienta-Konsultit Oy. Retrieved from http://lchc.ucsd.edu/MCA/Paper/Engestrom/expanding/toc.htm

Engeström, Y. (2001). Expansive learning at work: Toward an activity theoretical reconceptualization. *Journal of Education and Work, 14*(1), 133–156.

Ferguson, R., Clow, D., Macfadyen, L., Essa, A., Dawson, S., & Alexander, S. (2014). Setting learning analytics in context: Overcoming the barriers to large-scale adoption. *LAK14: Proceedings of the fourth international conference* on *learning analytics and knowledge* (pp. 251–253). http://dl.acm.org/citation. cfm?id=2567592

Flavin, M. (2016). Technology-enhanced learning and higher education. *Oxford Review of Economic Policy, 32*(4), 632–645.

Gasevic, D., Dawson, S., & Siemens, G. (2015). Let's not forget: Learning analytics are about learning. *TechTrends, 59*(1), 64–71.

Gikas, J., & Grant, M. M. (2013). Mobile computing devices in higher education: Student perspectives on learning with cellphones, smartphones and social media. *Internet and Higher Education, 19*, 18–26.

Gordon, N. (2014). *Flexible pedagogies: Technology-enhanced learning*. York: Higher Education Academy.

Head, A. J., & Eisenberg, M. B. (2010). How today's college students use Wikipedia for course-related research. *First Monday, 15*(3). Retrieved from http://firstmonday.org/ojs/index.php/fm/article/view/2830/2476

Hemmi, A., Bayne, S., & Land, R. (2009). The appropriation and repurposing of social technologies in higher education. *Journal of Computer Assisted Learning, 25*, 19–30.

Henderson, M., Selwyn, N., & Aston, R. (2015a). What works and why? Student perceptions of "useful" digital technology in university teaching and learning. *Studies in Higher Education*. doi:10.1080/03075079.2015a.1007946.

Henderson, M., Selwyn, N., Finger, G., & Aston, R. (2015b). Students' everyday engagement with digital technology in university: Exploring patterns of use and "usefulness". *Journal of Higher Education Policy and Management, 37*(3), 308–319.

Higher Education Funding Council for England (HEFCE). (2009). *Enhancing learning and teaching through the use of technology: A revised approach to HEFCE's strategy for e-learning*. Bristol: HEFCE.

Hillis, K., Petit, M., & Jarrett, K. (2013). *Google and the culture of search*. Abingdon: Routledge.

Horrigan, J.B. (2016). *Lifelong learning and technology*. Pew Research Center. Retrieved from http://www.pewinternet.org/2016/03/22/lifelong-learning-and-technology/

Jelfs, A., & Richardson, J. T. E. (2013). The use of digital technologies across the adult life span in distance education. *British Journal of Educational Technology, 44*(2), 338–351.

JISC. (2009). *Effective practice in a digital age: A guide to technology-enhanced learning and teaching*. Bristol: JISC.

Jisc. (2011). *Emerging practice in a digital age: A guide to technology-enhanced institutional innovation*. Bristol: Jisc.

Johnson, L., Adams-Becker, S., Cummins, M., Estrada, V., Freeman, A., & Hall, C. (2016). *NMC horizon report: 2016 higher education edition*. Austin: The New Media Consortium.

Jones, C. (2012). Networked learning, stepping beyond the net generation and digital natives. In L. Dirckinck-Holmfeld, V. Hodgson, & D. Mc Connell (Eds.), *Exploring the theory, pedagogy and practice of networked learning* (pp. 27–41). New York: Springer.

Jones, C., & Healing, G. (2010). Net generation students: Agency and choice and the new technologies. *Journal of Computer Assisted Learning, 26,* 344–356.

Jones, N., Blackley, H., Fitzgibbon, K., & Chew, E. (2010). Get out of MySpace! *Computers and Education, 54*(3), 776–782.

Kirkwood, A., & Price, L. (2014). Technology-enhanced learning and teaching in higher education: What is "enhanced" and how do we know? A critical literature review. *Learning, Media and Technology, 39*(1), 6–36.

Laurillard, D. (2007). Modelling benefits-oriented costs for technology enhanced learning. *Higher Education, 54,* 21–39.

Laurillard, D. (2016). The educational problem that MOOCs could solve: Professional development for teachers of disadvantaged students. *Research in Learning Technology, 24.* http://dx.doi.org/10.3402/rlt.v24.29369

Lave, J., & Wenger, E. (1991). *Situated learning: Legitimate peripheral participation.* Cambridge: Cambridge University Press.

Lawton, W., Ahmed, M., Angulo, T., Axel-Berg, A., Burrows, A., & Katsomitros, A. (2013). *Horizon scanning: What will higher education look like in 2020?* The Observatory on Borderless Higher Education. http://obhe.ac.uk/documents/view_details?id=929

Leontiev, A. N. (1978). *Activity, consciousness and personality* (trans. Hall, M.J.). Englewood Cliffs: Prentice Hall.

Leontiev, A. N. (1981). *Problems of the development of the mind.* Moscow: Progress.

Lepore, J. (2014). The disruption machine: What the Gospel of innovation gets wrong. *The New Yorker, 90*(17), 30–36.

Littlejohn, A., Beetham, H., & McGill, L. (2012). Learning at the digital frontier: A review of digital literacies in theory and practice. *Journal of Computer Assisted Learning, 28,* 547–556.

Madge, C., Meek, J., Wellens, J., & Hooley, T. (2009). Facebook, social integration and informal learning at university: It is more for socialising and talking to friends about work than for actually doing work. *Learning, Media and Technology, 34*(2), 141–155.

Margaryan, A., Littlejohn, A., & Vojt, G. (2011). Are digital natives a myth or reality? University students' use of digital technologies. *Computers and Education, 56,* 429–440.

O'Reilly, T. (2005). *What is Web 2.0: Design patterns and business models for the next generation of software.* O'Reilly. Retrieved from http://www.oreilly.com/pub/a/web2/archive/what-is-web-20.html

Prensky, M. (2001). Digital natives, digital immigrants. *On the Horizon, 9*(5). Retrieved from http://www.marcprensky.com/writing/prensky%20-%20digi tal%20natives,%20digital%20immigrants%20-%20part1.pdf

Rienties, B., Boroowa, A., Cross, S., Kubiak, C., Mayles, K., & Murphy, S. (2016). Analytics4Action evaluation framework: A review of evidence-based learning analytics interventions at the Open University UK. *Journal of Interactive Media in Education, 1*(2), 1–11.

Selwyn, N., & Gorard, S. (2016). Students' use of Wikipedia as an academic resource – Patterns of use and patterns of usefulness. *Internet and Higher Education, 28*, 28–34.

Siemens, G., & Gasevic, D. (2012). Guest editorial – Learning and knowledge analytics. *Educational Technology and Society, 15*(3), 1–2.

Sharples, M., Adams, A., Alozie, N., Ferguson, R., Fitzgerald, E., Gaved, M., McAndrew, P., Means, B., Remold, J., Rienties, B., Roschelle, J., Vogt, K., Whitelock, D., & Yarnall, L. (2015). *Innovating pedagogy 2015*. Milton Keynes: Open University.

Smith, P., Rao, L., & Thompson, S. (2013). *Towards developing a cost-benefit model for learning management systems*. CONF-IRM 2013: International Conference on Information Resources Management. Retrieved from http://aisel.aisnet. org/cgi/viewcontent.cgi?article=1045andcontext=confirm2013

Timmis, S. (2012). Constant companions: Instant messaging conversations as sustainable supportive study structures amongst undergraduate peers. *Computers and Education, 59*, 3–18.

Universities and Colleges Information Systems Association. (2014). *2014 survey of technology enhanced learning for higher education in the UK*. Oxford: University of Oxford.

Universities and Colleges Information Systems Association (UCISA). (2016). *2016 Survey of technology enhanced learning for higher education in the UK*. Oxford: University of Oxford.

Vygotsky, L. (1930). The socialist alteration of man. In R. Van Der Veet & J. Valsiner (Eds.), *The Vygotsky reader* (pp. 175–184). Oxford: Blackwell.

Wenger, E. (1998). *Communities of practice: Learning, meaning, and identity*. Cambridge: Cambridge University Press.

Yeap, J. A. L., Ramayah, T., & Soto-Acosta, P. (2016). Factors propelling the adoption of m-learning among students in higher education. *Electronic Markets*. doi:10.1007/s12525-015-0214-x.

Free, Simple and Easy to Use: Disruptive Technologies, Disruptive Innovation and Technology Enhanced Learning

INTRODUCTION

Disruptive Innovation describes a process whereby an innovation threatens and can dislodge an established market leader. It is used by Clayton Christensen as a lens to analyse a range of goods and services, from motor bikes to education (Christensen 1997; Christensen et al. 2008; Christensen and Eyring 2011).

The previous chapter identified and summarized the main ideas and arguments of the book. This chapter surveys research on Disruptive Innovation and discusses how it can be applied to technology enhanced learning. The primary focus of the chapter is the work of Christensen, but it is also interested in how the theory has been adapted and critiqued by other researchers. The aim of the chapter is to understand what is meant by disruptive technology and Disruptive Innovation and to identify the value and relevance of applying Disruptive Innovation to technology enhanced learning in higher education. The chapter argues that the purpose a technology attains is determined by practice rather than design and that the core, defining criteria of disruptive technologies are a useful means of analysing and anticipating the take up of technologies.

The chapter begins by examining the roots of Disruptive Innovation and also examines how the theory has been developed and critiqued. The chapter goes on to consider specific technologies and practices from the perspective of Disruptive Innovation. The chapter distinguishes between individual, disruptive technologies and the wider theory of Disruptive

© The Author(s) 2017
M. Flavin, *Disruptive Technology Enhanced Learning*,
DOI 10.1057/978-1-137-57284-4_2

Innovation. The chapter concludes by reviewing Disruptive Innovation and its relevance to a study of technology enhanced learning, while also anticipating the two other theoretical perspectives used in the book, namely, Activity Theory and expansive learning, and the Community of Practice theory.

CLAYTON CHRISTENSEN AND DISRUPTIVE INNOVATION

Bower and Christensen first published on disruptive technologies and Disruptive Innovation in the *Harvard Business Review* in 1995, arguing that disruptive technologies, 'typically present a different package of performance attributes – ones that, at least at the outset, are not valued by existing customers' (p. 44). The newness of disruptive technologies comprises the challenge of disruptive technologies because, initially, users can be unclear about what to do with them; the purpose for the technology, and thus its market, arises through practice. Bower and Christensen (1995) recommend that established firms should create organizations separate from the main business to challenge the impact of disruptive technologies on their markets, a view Christensen continued to advocate (Christensen 1997; Christensen and Raynor 2003). Such an approach would be challenging to universities because of its potential to dilute a brand, but it has been adopted in some quarters to develop Massive Open Online Courses (MOOCs); Harvard and MIT combined to develop edX and, in the UK, FutureLearn was created by the Open University to develop MOOCs.

Bower and Christensen (1995) argue that established firms are ill-placed to take on disruptive technologies because doing so involves a radical departure from existing practice (p. 48). An example they provide is the Polaroid camera; market researchers had wrongly estimated sales of only 100,000 units over the product's lifetime, because the researchers' interviewees were unable to imagine uses for instant photography. Purposes for the technology were created through practice, assisted by distribution channels which moved the product away from its traditional customer base; Tripsas and Gavetti (2000) show how Polaroid was radical for its time by distributing its products through K-Mart and Walmart rather than through specialist camera shops. Christensen and Eyring (2011) later note that innovating on behalf of a customer is difficult (p. 331); disruptive technologies often create new markets rather than rely on existing customers. It is worth noting that Polaroid itself ceased trading in 2008, having been disrupted by digital photography.

Christensen presents a fuller discussion of his theory in a book of 1997. He writes about goods and services and constructs a dualism between technologies that enable us to do something we had already been doing a little better than before (sustaining) and technologies that prompt new forms of practice (disruptive). In a later book, he gives examples of sustaining technologies: 'Airplanes that fly farther, computers that process faster, cellular phone batteries that last longer, and televisions with clearer images' (Christensen et al. 2008, p. 46).

Disruptive technologies often start with a small number of users, but grow over time to the extent that they can displace a previously dominant, incumbent technology:

> What all sustaining technologies have in common is that they improve the performance of established products... Disruptive technologies bring to market a very different value proposition than had been available previously... Products based on disruptive technologies are typically cheaper, simpler, smaller, and, frequently, more convenient to use. (Christensen 1997, p. xv)

The distinction between the two categories can be more complex than it appears at first. Christensen and Raynor (2003) cite the example of the electronic cash register, which was a significant step up technologically from the electromechanical cash register but which did the same job, only more efficiently (p. 40). The practice stayed the same; therefore, the electronic cash register was a sustaining innovation.

Disruptive technologies typically enable new markets to emerge, a point Christensen (1997) develops: 'when they [disruptive technologies] initially emerge, neither manufacturers nor customers know how or why the products will be used... Building such markets entails a process of mutual discovery by customers and manufacturers – and this simply takes time' (p. 135). Christensen (1997) also argues that innovation comes from the ground up (p. 82), an argument repeated by Christensen and Raynor (2003). Relating Christensen's core thesis to technology enhanced learning, innovation can come from students who arrive at universities as new entrants and who bring their pre-existing practices with technologies with them, but it is up to more senior figures, and to the university itself on an institutional level, to decide what to do about disruptive technologies, whether to welcome or prohibit their usage.

One of Christensen's (1997) case studies is the Honda motor cycle in the USA. Honda had built its business successfully in Japan between 1949 and

1959 through its small, 50 cc Super Cub bike, before developing a bike for the USA market based on size, power and speed. The bike failed to break into the USA market. However, the Super Cub was suitable for off-road recreational use and Honda created a market by selling the Super Cub through sporting goods retailers rather than motor bike dealers. Having thus gained a foothold in the market by selling to what Christensen and Raynor (2003) call, 'people without leather jackets' (p. 252), Honda was able to develop along sustaining lines (the typical, long-term trajectory of Disruptive Innovation which becomes sustaining innovation) by building progressively more powerful bikes (1997, pp. 154–5). Christensen (1997) shows how Honda had a product which was cheap, simple, small and convenient, and created a market for it; the Super Cub acquired the purpose of off-road, recreational biking through practice. Hart and Christensen (2002) suggest Honda's strategy was typical of the Japanese economy in the post-World War II era and was also practised by Toyota and Sony, stressing low prices and simplicity. In effect, 'Disruption was the nation's strategy of national economic development' (p. 52).

Disruptive Innovation creates communities of users by offering simplicity, convenience and affordability and by offering a product or service that the community had not had access to previously. The means by which the goods or services are made available is also important; Christensen and Raynor (2003) argue, 'Disruptive products require disruptive channels' (p. 119). Similarly, many technologies used to support learning and teaching by students and lecturers are not made available through universities, but are more convenient and easy to use than universities' proprietary technologies. Disruptive technologies help students and lecturers to get jobs done.

Christensen and Raynor (2003) amplify an argument set out by Christensen (1997), namely, that the likely success of a disruptive technology relates to the circumstances of innovation; in sustaining circumstances, the incumbent is likely to prevail over the disruptor, but in disruptive circumstances the innovator is likely to prevail over the incumbent (Christensen and Raynor 2003, p. 32). Disruption is not an intrinsic feature of a technology. Christensen and Raynor's argument underlines the importance of practice in Disruptive Innovation, because practice produces purpose. Activity Theory (see Chap. 3) helps disentangle Disruptive Innovation in this regard, as second generation Activity Theory names specific social circumstances or variables (rules, community and the division of labour) that have a determining effect on a technology's outcomes. Universities are durable institutions and thus may be prone to maintaining sustaining circumstances, but the potential of technology enhanced learning nurtures the potential for more substantial transformation. When rapid technological development is combined with shifting economic changes in higher education, such as rapid growth in tuition fees in many countries, disruptive circumstances may arise.

Christensen and Raynor (2003) sub-divide Disruptive Innovation. New-market disruptions compete with non-consumption, making goods or services available to a constituency who had previously not had access to them. Low-end disruptions involve the innovator coming in at the bottom end of an established market. Both new-market and low-end disruptive innovations can be successful, because incumbents ignore the former and move away from the latter as they cater to their high-end and more profitable customers. From this perspective, and relating the principle to higher education, new students bringing their technology practices to a university can be low-end disruptors, as they have not been socialized into the university community and use the convenient, non-institutional technologies with which they are already familiar. Universities may disregard the newcomers' practices and focus on their proprietal technologies in order to defend their established model of practice, but in so doing they may not be attuned to the actual technology practices of their own students.

Christensen and Raynor (2003) demonstrate how purpose and practice relate to each other.

> When customers become aware of a job that they need to get done in their lives, they look around for a product or service that they can 'hire' to get the job done. This is how customers experience life. Their thought processes originate with an awareness of needing to get something done, and then they set out to hire something or someone to do the job as effectively, conveniently, and inexpensively as possible... Companies that target their products at the *circumstances* in which the customers find themselves, rather than at the customers themselves, are those that can launch predictably successful products. Put another way, the critical unit of analysis is the *circumstance* and *not the customer*. (2003, p. 75, emphasis in original)

Christensen and Raynor (2003) summarize their approach as 'a jobs-to-be-done' lens (p. 79); technologies are used to accomplish specific purposes. These purposes may not conflate with the technology designer's intentions but this is not important because purpose is constructed, not preordained.

A case study cited frequently by Christensen is the Sony transistor radio (Bower and Christensen 1995; Christensen and Raynor 2003; Christensen et al. 2008): 'in 1955, Sony introduced the first battery-powered, pocket transistor radio. In comparison with the big RCA tabletop radios, the Sony pocket radio was tinny and static-laced. But Sony chose to sell its transistor radio to nonconsumers – teenagers who could not afford a big tabletop radio.' Therefore, 'because Sony deployed the transistor against nonconsumption, all it had to do was make a product that was better than nothing' (Christensen et al. 2008, pp. 80–1). The product was affordable to a constituency who could not afford radios previously (teenagers), which helped to produce new forms of broadcasting practice, as programmes were made to appeal to the newly-enfranchised community. (To the fullest of my knowledge, no one has written a PhD on the Sony transistor radio as a causal factor in the invention of rock and roll, but it is probably only a matter of time.) A new technology, the transistor radio, catalysed new forms of practice, which determined the evolution of the technology and the supersedence of the table top radio by the transistor radio. The transistor radio thereafter became a sustaining technology and was disrupted in turn by radio over the internet, which disrupted the transistor radio on the same terms that the transistor radio disrupted the table top radio (Naughton 2012, p. 108). Sony applied the same principle to the introduction of their black-and-white portable television in 1959, which appealed to apartment-dwellers lacking the space for a large, domestic television (Christensen and Raynor 2003, pp. 104–5). In both cases, the product created a new market, from which its market position grew. The transistor itself was invented not by Sony but by AT and T, but it was Sony who saw the potential for a pocket radio which, while inferior in sound quality, brought the technology to previous non-consumers.

Disruption works, not by confronting established practice but by offering something new, delivered through an unexpected channel: Christensen et al. (2008) argue, 'A major lesson from our studies of innovation is that disruptive innovation does not take root through a direct attack on the existing system. Instead, it must go around and underneath the system' (p. 225). Applying technology enhanced learning within established pedagogic models can be problematic because the technology gets manipulated to suit the existing pedagogy and thus only a small portion of the learning and teaching potential of the technology is realized. The technology confronts an existing pedagogical model and gets consumed by it. Therefore, and in order to utilize the full potential of technology enhanced learning, universities need to observe what technologies can do, what students and lecturers actually do with technologies and align these practices with course content, assessment and delivery. If technology can make learning available to people who do not currently have easy access to higher education, then the extent of the education offered will initially be less significant than the fact that it is being offered at all. Marginalized communities and developing countries may not have easy access to higher education, but technology can make it available to anyone with access to a networked device and thus technology has disruptive potential, though Laurillard (2013) has argued that democratising access to resources is not the same as access to education, and the effective use of disruptive technologies in technology enhanced learning is predicated on sufficient network bandwidth and on the technology infrastructure in general, as noted in a case study of technology enhanced learning in three universities in Tanzania (Mahenge and Sanga 2016). It is not the aim of this book to explore the potential of disruptive technologies to widen global access to higher education, though research has been undertaken in this area (for example, Ng'ambi 2013; Rambe and Nel 2015). Instead, this book is focused on understanding how universities can engage constructively with disruptive technologies in higher education, and Christensen and his co-authors argue for the specific conditions best suited to the adoption of a disruptive technology.

Christensen has described disruptive innovations and sustaining innovations and has added a third category of efficiency innovations (Denning 2016), which make it possible to do more with less; efficiency innovations can therefore be a threat to jobs in higher education. Technology enhanced learning can be applied to all three of Christensen's revised categories; new technological possibilities can comprise disruptive innovations, sustaining innovations comprise the ongoing development of existing technologies, and efficiency innovations are distinct because they are potentially pedagogically constrictive and can threaten academic practice from the opposite end of the scale to disruptive innovations, though efficiency innovations also offer economies of scale. Christensen et al. (2016) argue that efficiency innovations 'reduce cost by eliminating labor or by redesigning products to eliminate components or replace them with cheaper alternatives,' but acknowledge that the approach can lead to 'a race to the bottom.' Skarzynski and Rufat-Latre (2011) note that low growth and high unemployment are conducive to Disruptive Innovation in many fields, offering goods and services at lower cost (p. 5). However, by using technologies to enable higher student to staff ratios, a transmissive curriculum ensues, militating against the co-creation of knowledge by students and lecturers. Moreover, efficiency innovation can impact on universities' library services, as web-based tools can supplant academic librarians. In addition, costly specialist databases can get superseded by Google Scholar and similar applications; as Karlsson (2014) notes, and in addition to the simplicity, ease of use and convenience of Google Scholar, it corrects misspellings, unlike many specialist databases (p. 1663). Efficiency innovation can result in streamlined practices enabling jobs to be done, but at the same time it poses a threat to academic jobs if the rationale underpinning efficiency innovation is solely concerned with doing more with less.

Similar criticism relating to a transmissive pedagogy may be made of iTunesU which, as Tseng et al. (2016) argue, tends to be characterized by static content without social interaction, resulting in 'mundane courses' (p. 199). The innovation is sustaining, offering an alternative platform from which to access learning materials, but not rethinking learning and teaching or causing radically different forms of practice. Instead, transmissive teaching is relocated to the online environment. Therefore, while it is a truism to state that technologies have changed aspects of learning and teaching, the nature of the innovation is unclear; innovation can threaten academic practice through efficiency innovation rather than enhance it, or limit the pedagogical impact of technology enhanced leaning through sustaining innovation.

Christensen et al. (2008) argue that the school education system in the USA has relied on sustaining technologies, and Christensen and Eyring (2011) claim that higher education, too, has adhered to the sustaining technology approach: 'Since the time that universities first gathered students into classrooms, the learning technologies... have remained largely the same. Even when computers were introduced into the classroom, they were used to enhance the existing instructional approaches, rather than to supplant them. Lectures, for example, were augmented with computer graphics, but the lecture itself persisted in its fundamental form' (p. 18). Disruptive Innovation faces an uphill task in higher education, but disruptive technologies are being used on a daily basis by students and lecturers to support their learning and teaching, which suggests a tension between the university as an institution on one hand, and the practices of students and lecturers on the other.

Christensen et al. (2015) argue for the predictive value of Disruptive Innovation, a position Christensen has held consistently: 'Disruption is a theory: a conceptual model of cause and effect that makes it possible to better predict the outcomes of competitive battles in different circumstances' (Christensen and Raynor 2003, p. 55). However, Christensen et al. (2015) also emphasize the principle that disruption is a process, not an event. The process can take a long time, up to decades, to unfold, and therefore the predictive potential of the theory cannot be evaluated in the short term. A further problem is that some predictions associated with Disruptive Innovation have not been borne out. For example, Christensen and Raynor (2003) argued it was unlikely that customers would want cameras integrated with their phones (p. 85). The predictive potential of Disruptive Innovation, as argued for by Christensen, is not enhanced by actual predictions Christensen has made. Christensen (2006) asserts, 'the value of a theory is assessed by its predictive power' (p. 42), but if this precept were to be applied rigidly, his own theory would emerge with a chequered record.

One of the case studies Christensen et al. (2015) present underlines the relationship between practice and design in disruption. They cite the Apple iPhone, a sustaining technology as far as smartphones were concerned, but disruptive in challenging the laptop or desktop as means of accessing the internet. The iPhone is also a 'premium product' (Denning 2016), which does not conform to the idea of new technologies entering at the bottom end of the market. The iPhone enables disruption through its ease of use, encouraging experimentation on the part of users; the iPhone and similar devices are portable and provide quick and easy access to the internet, thus comprising a disruptive technology. Pisano (2015) argues, 'Apple consistently focuses its innovation on making its products easier to use than competitors' (p. 7), implying the potential for Disruptive Innovation in Apple's approach to product design. However, Apple products are not always wholly innovative; Chena et al. (2016) argue that Apple's iPad was preceded by tablet computers from both Hewlett Packard and Dell, but it was Apple who achieved market success (p. 563). The success of Apple products where similar, competitors' products failed implies that marketing and branding play a part in the success of disruptive technologies (see Markides 2006, below).

It is also worth noting Christensen's earlier scepticism concerning the disruptive potential of the iPhone: 'The iPhone is a sustaining technology relative to Nokia. In other words, Apple is leaping ahead on the sustaining curve [by building a better phone]. But the prediction of the theory would be that Apple won't succeed with the iPhone. They've launched an innovation that the existing players in the industry are heavily motivated to beat: It's not [truly] disruptive. History speaks pretty loudly on that, that the probability of success is going to be limited' (McGregor 2007). Christensen's defence of this apparently poor prediction would probably be that disruption is a process and not an event, but the prediction complicates and compromises the predictive potential of Disruptive Innovation and can be used to support the argument of Lepore (2014) and Danneels (2004, 2006) that Disruptive Innovation is weakened by its use of the retrospective case study as its methodology. Lepore (2014) argues that Disruptive Innovation make a poor prophet. It is easy to agree, but this book argues that Christensen's core criteria for a disruptive technology (cheap, simple, small and convenient) are consistently useful starting points for appraising technology adoption.

THE TECHNOLOGY ADOPTION MODEL

Disruptive Innovation is not without precedent. The Technology Adoption Model (Davis 1989) argues that perceived usefulness (the ability of a technology to get a job done) and perceived ease of use ('the degree to which a person believes that using a particular system would be free of effort' (p. 320)) shape the adoption of technologies. The model is simple, and therefore lucid, but it is also reductive. Bagozzi (2007) identifies the 'parsimony' (p. 244) of the Technology Acceptance Model as both a strength and a weakness; a strength because it posits a causal and linear relationship between perceived usefulness and perceived ease of use on one hand, and intentions to use on the other; a weakness because of its reductiveness. Subsequently, Edmunds et al. (2012) argue for the importance of usefulness and ease of use in technology adoption, especially in work settings, though they too note the reductiveness of the model (p. 72). If, as Edmunds et al. (2012) suggest, the context of work is especially relevant in assessing the likely take up of technologies by users, the significant numbers of students taking up paid employment during their higher education studies (Robotham (2012) found 67% of students working, from a research sample of 1827 at a UK university, while Sodexo (2016) found 28% of students working while studying, in a sample of 2000+ students across the UK) may create the conditions in which work-based experiences of technologies become prime determinants shaping technology usage in higher education as technologies cross borders between the workplace and university, though the integration of non-institutional technologies may also suggest that universities are lagging behind in terms of making new and useful technologies readily available to students and lecturers. Edmunds et al.'s (2012) 'perceived usefulness at work' determinant can be related to Christensen and Raynor's (2003) 'jobs to be done' lens. In both cases, technologies appeal because of their demonstrable use value.

While acknowledging the applicability of the Technology Acceptance Model as a general guide to understanding technology adoption in education, the Disruptive Innovation approach is a more useful and more illuminating lens for this book because Disruptive Innovation's primary focus is on both the technology and practice with the technology, with emphasis on the latter. Disruptive Innovation hones in on practice with the technology being used more than it focuses on the individual human subject undertaking the usage. This stress is relevant because Activity Theory, which is also used in this book (Chap. 3), argues against the idea of the human subject as unique and inviolable, thereby implicitly challenging psychological interpretations of technology adoption because it questions the idea of stable and immutable selfhood. Instead, Activity Theory argues that the human subject, in terms of its consciousness, is a product of historical and social forces. It is a core tenet of this book that practice is social as, indeed, is identity. Innovation, therefore, does not occur in a vacuum but in contexts which both open up and circumscribe parameters of innovation. This is not to denigrate other approaches, but to serve this book's coherence; the theoretical approaches used in this book view identity, practice and innovation as ultimately social phenomena. It is therefore internally coherent for this book to adopt the Disruptive Innovation approach, because it directs the analysis more towards practice with the technology tool than towards the subject undertaking the usage, though this book is also interested in the interactions, the intertraffic, between subjects and technologies, but not in the subject in isolation, nor in the subject as a primary or all-determining explanation for technology adoption.

From a Technology Acceptance Model perspective, Davis (1989) argues, 'the prominence of usefulness over ease of use has important implications for designers' (p. 334), but Disruptive Innovation argues that practice takes priority over design in determining purpose: to deploy an analogy, practice is the base and design the superstructure. This book uses the four criteria set down by Christensen (1997) and the more developed understanding of Disruptive Innovation put forward by Christensen and Raynor (2003) to analyse the adoption of technologies, seeing practice as primary in determining purpose. Bagozzi (2007) argues, 'more is needed in TAM [Technology Acceptance Model] explicitly focusing on end-state goals/objectives of technology use' (p. 245). This book is able to focus on the objectives of technology use through the blending of the disruptive technology approach with Activity Theory, which has the objects (purposes) to which technology use is directed as one of its core concerns. Therefore, through its focus on objects, in the sense of purposes, Activity Theory enables a particular form of analysis which is less prevalent within the Technology Acceptance Model.

COMMENTARY ON AND CRITIQUE OF DISRUPTIVE INNOVATION

Govindarajan and Kopalle (2006) develop Christensen's initial framework by focusing on a distinction between radical innovations and disruptive innovations. Radical innovations are about technologies whereas disruptive innovations are about practice and market behaviour. Govindarajan and Kopalle (2006) conclude that enabling disruptive innovations presupposes some risk-taking and failure. Consequently, identifying disruption is essentially reactive, echoing the analysis of Christensen and Raynor (2003) and Christensen (2006).

Govindarajan et al. (2011) argue that disruptive innovations do not necessarily involve the newest technology (unlike radical innovations), but often involve a willingness to cannibalize and an ability to appeal to an emerging market segment. They conclude: 'firms that are focused narrowly on serving current customers will not have disruptive innovations, potentially putting them at risk from such innovations introduced by competitors' (p. 130), which echoes the position outlined by Christensen (1997) and Christensen and Raynor (2003). Relating this argument to higher education and without a shift in the demographics of the population entering higher education, there may be little immediate and obvious incentive to innovate. However, as financial support from government for higher education recedes (Lawton et al. (2013) note, 'The gradual withdrawal of the state from HE funding in developed countries is set to stay' (p. 43)), universities will incur pressure to take on more of the qualities of businesses without diluting their fundamental character. Engaging with the technology practices of students and lecturers is one route to innovate, realizing the potential to enhance learning and teaching without compromising the mission of the university.

Moore (2004) argues that disruptive innovation 'tends to have its roots in technological discontinuities, such as the one that enabled Motorola's rise to prominence with the first generation of cell phones, or in fast-spreading fads like the collector game Pokémon' (p. 88). Moore's argument aligns with Christensen's (1997) original formulation of disruptive technology, but the mention of fads hones in usefully on the idea that not all disruptions are sustainable. Furthermore, disruption is not necessarily good; Cortez (2014) identifies 'novel securities instruments' (p. 185) that contributed to the 2008 financial crisis as a disruptive innovation, and Lepore (2014) adds, 'When the financial-services industry disruptively innovated, it led to a global financial crisis.' Disruption is a form of practice, and how it develops depends on how communities create a purpose for a disruptive technology. However, this is not necessarily a benign process and it is not an organic process, as features such as marketing or entrenched practices can shape a community's and an individual's response to a technology.

Moore (2004) comes up with another category, Application Innovation, and supplies the example of hole-in-the-wall cash machines, an outcome of the invention of fault tolerant computers (p. 88). This is very close to Disruptive Innovation, which sees disruption arising from practice rather than design. Fault tolerant computers were not designed a priori to enable ATM machines but found a valuable purpose in that area. Moore's use of Application Innovation suggests that innovation can be a conscious process (at the application if not the design stage) whereas Christensen and Raynor (2003) see innovation as more serendipitous, arising out of practice.

While Moore looks to sub-divide disruption, Markides (2006) argues that disruption can occur through planning as well as through practice. Markides identifies sub-categories of innovation, including disruptive business model innovation and disruptive product innovation. Disruptive business model innovations attract new customers or persuade existing customers to consume more (p. 26). For example, Amazon is a business model innovator, as it introduced a new business model that attracted customers: 'Amazon did not discover bookselling; it redefined what the service is all about, what the customer gets out of it, and how the service is provided to the customer' (p. 20). Markides also argues that business model innovations gain a certain percentage of the market, but, contrary to Christensen, do not remove incumbents (p. 21), citing the case studies of internet banking and no frills airlines, both of which exist alongside their predecessors. The decline of High Street banking in the UK suggests that online banking as a disruptive technology has improved its performance along sustaining technology lines since its introduction, and that the marketing of online banking (for example, HSBC's subsidiary, First Direct, an entirely online bank founded by the then Midland Bank in 1989) has played a role in the spread of the disruption. However, Christensen and Raynor

(2003) argue online banking is a sustaining innovation relative to orthodox retail banking (p. 201); in common with the introduction of the electronic cash register (discussed earlier), the core practice remains the same. Markides (2008) argues that First Direct was kept as separate as possible from the established bank, thus following Christensen's advice to incumbents on how to deal with disruption, by creating an autonomous subsidiary with the freedom to create its own practices. That said, the convenience of online banking does mean it shares some characteristics with Christensen's original formulation of a disruptive technology. The resilience, or at least clear survival, albeit on a reduced scale, of High Street banking suggests there is something about the human interface which produces value in itself, a possibility universities might want to consider before moving to wholly online models of delivery and support. Lorange and Rembiszewski (2016) state that Facebook and Google have banking licenses (p. 15), but there are no signs of them seeking to displace established names in banking. There may therefore be something significant about brands in banking, as in higher education, that underlines and nurtures reputation.

Markides (2006) defines Christensen's disruptive technologies creating new markets as disruptive product innovations. He gives the car and mobile phones as examples. He further argues that these innovations are not, in general, driven by demand, but by supply (p. 22), which aligns with Christensen, who sees the disruption arising from individuals' interactions with new technologies, leading to new practices disrupting established markets. In terms of who prospers and who fails in these conditions, Markides (2006) argues that successful participants time their entry into the market. Markides (2006) also argues that disruptive product innovations develop strong brands, control the channels of distribution and thus build from a niche into the mass market. Markides (2006) therefore steers understandings of innovation away from ideas of unfettered, spontaneous creativity and towards an understanding of innovation as structured and planned within existing market practices and behaviours, and thus malleable through effective product development and marketing. Markides (2006) also stresses the importance of brand, which is also relevant in a stratified higher education market; in the UK, for example, the Russell Group of universities comprises a selective club of research-led institutions.

Markides's (2006) reading of Disruptive Innovation is distinctive because he argues it can be created consciously and through pre-planning. Furthermore, his analysis can be applied to broader practices with technologies. For example, in learning and teaching, and in other areas of practice,

Second Life (a virtual world in which people adopt new identities, known as avatars) was innovative, yet, despite widespread publicity, did not gain a substantial foothold in higher education as, in practice, it was not used extensively and was unable to build a sustainable niche (Livingstone 2011); an Organization for Economic Co-operation and Development study in the USA (2009, p. 15) found that less than 9% of students used Second Life or other virtual worlds. Individual case studies of the successful adoption of Second Life in higher education have been undertaken (for example, Zold 2014; Reinsmith-Jones et al. 2015), but Second Life has not proved to be a successful disruptive technology in higher education as a whole because Second Life has not disrupted established practices in higher education, perhaps because it takes the user some time to gain competence in it; Second Life does not have the immediacy and obvious use value of an internet search engine. A similar failure was experienced previously by the Stanford Centre for Research, Development and Teaching which was tech-nologically advanced for its time, but led by technology rather than practice (Cuban 2001, pp. 99–101) and, again, proved to be an unsustainable innovation. In both cases, the innovation was technology-led rather than practice-led, and practice is the key determinant of disruption.

In Disruptive Innovation, users construct a meaning for a technology which may differ from the designer's original intentions. Smagorinsky's (2001) analysis of the construction of meaning adds complexity by arguing that the construction of meaning is not an unfettered process and, instead, is shaped by pre-existing power structures in a society (p. 136). Smagorinsky (2001) argues that the possibilities of meaning are shaped by individuals' historical and cultural inheritance, an argument which aligns with Vygotsky (see Chap. 3). In practice, in learning and teaching situations, 'teachers emphasize specific reading conventions and discourage others' (p. 138), an argument which can be extended to the institutional advocacy of the use of specific technologies. Consequently, socio-economic groups socialized within the dominant culture have an educational advantage, as their values and practices have already been constructed and reaffirmed by the dominant culture.

Smagorinsky's (2001) understanding of knowledge overlaps with Wenger's (1998) when the latter writes, 'Our knowing – even of the most unexceptional kind – is always too big, too rich, too ancient, and too connected for us to be the source of it individually' (p. 141 (see Chap. 4)). Therefore, when users use technologies in innovative, disruptive ways, it is helpful to understand users' prior social experiences; Christensen (1997) and Christensen and Raynor (2003) argue that innovation comes from the ground up. Disruptive technology use occurs, but some disruptions are more welcome than others. One possibility is that innovation comes from the ground up but it also comes from those who do not form part of, or who reject, the dominant culture. In this sense, innovation is disruptive by definition when it emerges from people who are not inculcated with existing, dominant values and practices.

Blin and Munro (2008) critique the impact of technology on learning and teaching in higher education, arguing technology has not changed pedagogy. They use Activity Theory as the primary lens for their analysis but Disruptive Innovation is relevant too. Blin and Munro's research suggests it is challenging to consciously create a disruptive technology in higher education because the disruption emerges through practice and is not an intrinsic feature of the technology itself. What can be attempted, however, is a creation of the circumstances in which disruption can happen. This involves a receptive and accommodating approach to the use of technologies for learning, even when those technologies are not explicitly technologies for learning. It may further involve the kind of conscious market manipulation suggested by Markides (2006), with students and lecturers being made aware of the learning and teaching possibilities of disruptive technologies.

The fiercest criticism of Disruptive Innovation has come from another Harvard professor, Jill Lepore. In a 2014 article in the *New Yorker*, she describes Disruptive Innovation as a 'competitive strategy for an age seized by terror' and 'a theory of history founded on a profound anxiety about financial collapse, and apocalyptic fear of global devastation, and shaky evidence,' gaining ubiquity 'only after 9/11.' The focus of Christensen's work, however, is on innovation in relation to goods and services. Consequently, to extrapolate from Christensen's argument to a global context without nuance is problematic, as it is not a full and fair reflection of Christensen's actual position. The same might be said of applying Disruptive Innovation to technology enhanced learning in higher education, but Christensen and his co-authors have applied Disruptive Innovation to education, including higher education (2008, 2011), without the theory creaking under the strain (see also, Flavin 2016b).

Lepore's argument is stronger when she criticizes Christensen's evidence. Christensen uses, as Lepore phrases it, 'handpicked case studies.' Therefore, Christensen is able to retrospectively pick case studies that validate his core argument. In this specific sense Christensen's approach is problematic. However, this book is less interested in Christensen's work as an expression of absolute truth than it is in the use of Disruptive Innovation as a tool, in an Activity Theory sense (see Chap. 3); the theory comprises a lens through which we can view technology enhanced learning from a different perspective, a perspective enabling us to see errors that have been made in relation to technology enhanced learning in higher education and to propose means by which we can avoid making the same errors in future. This book, therefore, is not the elucidation of a single theory. Instead, it applies different but complementary theoretical perspectives as lenses through which to examine technology enhanced learning in higher education.

In common with Danneels (2006), Lepore points to the failure of the Disruptive Growth Fund, launched with Christensen's involvement in 2000, designed to fund emerging disruptive innovations and which closed within a year, having lost 64% of its value, compared to an overall stock exchange fall of 50%. Christensen is vulnerable on this point, too. Danneels (2006) seeks to excuse the failure of the Disruptive Growth Fund, arguing it was established when the technology bubble was at its most inflated (by the way, shouldn't Christensen have predicted that?), and Christensen (Bennett 2014) has downplayed his involvement with the Disruptive Growth Fund. However, it remains a blemish on his theory.

Lepore argues, 'schools, colleges and universities, churches, museums, and many hospitals, all of which have been subjected to disruptive innovation, have revenues and expenses and infrastructures, but they aren't industries in the same way that manufacturers of hard-disk drives or truck engines or dry goods are industries.' The point is a truism, but a truism worth making, because Disruptive Innovation can, in theory at least, be applied to a whole range of practices, not all of which will be valid applications of the theory. However, having criticized the unproblematic, reductive application of Disruptive Innovation, Lepore compares Disruptive Innovation, reductively, to startup companies: 'The logic of disruptive innovation is the logic of the startup: establish a team of innovators, set a whiteboard under a blue sky, and never ask them to make a profit, because there needs to be a wall of separation between the people whose job it is to come up with the best, smartest and most creative and important ideas and the people whose job it is to make money by selling stuff.' She develops the comparison still further:

The upstarts who work at startups don't often stay at one place for very long. (Three out of four startups fail. More than nine out of ten never earn a return.) They work a year here, a few months there – zany hours everywhere. They

wear jeans and sneakers and ride scooters and share offices and sprawl on couches like Great Danes. Their coffee machines look like dollhouse-size factories.

They sound like really quite annoying people to work with, but that is not the point. The point is that Disruptive Innovation is seen as a paper-thin, ethereal practice, academically unsound and inadequately supported by poor data and hype. That said, the ease with which Lepore constructs the comparison leads to her being reductive, just as she criticizes Disruptive Innovation for being reductive.

Lepore's assault on Disruptive Innovation cannot be dismissed out of hand, and Christensen's evidence base, characterized by the handpicked case study, is problematic. However, this book is interested in Disruptive Innovation for its identification of core criteria for disruptive technologies and for its insistence on practice as foundational in the construction of purpose. Moreover, the distinction between sustaining and disruptive technologies enables us to flag practices with technologies that have transformative potential on a higher education sectoral level.

Having reviewed Disruptive Innovation and commentaries on and critiques of Disruptive Innovation, a number of technologies and practices are now reviewed from a Disruptive Innovation perspective.

GOOGLE

Google is a disruptive technology. It is convenient, simple and free. Furthermore, purposes for the use of Google are constructed by its users. Designers provide the platform but do not dictate the practice. However, as Google has grown, it has developed niche products and services, offering a range of tools from specialist academic searches to document composition and storage and thus developing its disruptive technology along sustaining technology lines. Christensen et al. (2008) argue that disruptive innovations become sustaining innovations over time, an argument made more recently regarding technology enhanced learning by Yamagata-Lynch et al. (2015).

However, some of Google's innovations have failed. Google Wave, for example, was launched in 2009 enabling real-time collaboration and communication but was discontinued in 2010, and Google Buzz, Google's in-house social networking facility, was launched in 2010 and discontinued in 2011 (Hillis et al. 2013, p. 3). Moreover, Christensen et al. (2016) argue that Google+ is failing, because 'consumers apparently didn't see the value from combining search and social networking; to the consumer, the jobs are very different and arise in different circumstances in their lives.' These technologies provided by Google exemplify a feature of Disruptive Innovation in the sense that a technology fails when it is unable to attain a clear and distinct purpose through practice. Users already had technologies to communicate and to network and thus Google's innovations in this regard offered nothing new to users, nor a marked improvement on what they already had. Consequently, a notable aspect of disruptive technologies is that they are often multifaceted, or at least pliable enough to readily enable repurposing; the purpose of the technology is constructed by the user, and can vary from user to user. Twitter, for example, can be used to transmit, trivialize or troll.

In my own research, an observation study of seven participants showed the participants opting for easy and convenient technologies to accomplish a given task (finding information to support an academic assignment); six of the participants used Google, and the participant who did not use Google did use Google Scholar (Flavin 2015). Google was the first source used by five of the participants. One participant entered terms in a search box on her university's home page. The results came up provided by Bing. The participant clicked off Bing without looking at the results and entered the same search terms on Google (pp. 6–7). It appeared the participant had a preferred brand, in line with Markides's (2006) analysis of disruptive technologies and their uptake. Furthermore, participants in the research did not look beyond the first two pages of results on Google (five out of the seven did not look beyond the first page), though it is worth noting that it was a time-limited study. Similarly, Lawrence (2015) states that the students in her research rarely looked beyond the first page of results on Google. Resources are sought quickly by users and convenience is prioritized. Technologies that meet clear needs and priorities dovetail effectively with users' requirements.

WIKIPEDIA

Further research I undertook through a survey sought to identify the extent of participants' awareness of technologies and the purposes for which they used them (Flavin 2012, 2016a). Survey participants used a small range of technologies to accomplish a wide range of tasks, with the tendency being to use disruptive technologies. Wikipedia was used widely by the participants. In a separate study, Selwyn and Gorard (2016) show students to be efficient users of Wikipedia, 'fulfilling a supplementary and/or introductory role, providing students with initial orientation and occasional clarification on topics and concepts which they would subsequently research more thoroughly elsewhere' (p. 33). Furthermore, Tossell et al. (2015), in a study of the use of smartphones in higher education, found that 83% of their sample of 24 students downloaded Wikipedia Mobile. Wikipedia is a disruptive technology because it has disrupted the way knowledge is distributed and the way knowledge is produced, with collaborative production replacing the sole, acknowledged expert. Wikipedia is also a disruptive technology because it has dislodged an established incumbent through Wikipedia's convenience, ease of use and through the fact that it is free, its content produced by some of its users; it is worth noting that Encyclopaedia Britannica stopped publishing in print form in 2012, its mode of publication having been surpassed by the disruptive technology. The printed encyclopedia is a sustaining technology, updating its contents along established lines and publication formats but finding it difficult to compete with an online encyclopedia which is free and available to anyone with a networked device, although individual entries on Wikipedia can be seen as progressing along sustaining lines, as they are updated by contributors, thus repeating the pattern of initial disruption followed by incremental and sustainable improvement identified by Christensen (1997).

One participant in my survey stated, 'the biggest advantage of Wikipedia is that the answers are at your fingertips, you can ask a question and the answer appears without the need for flicking from chapter to chapter in a book' (Flavin 2016a, b, p. 9). In addition, Lawrence (2015) argues 'traditional rules don't apply' (p. 89) to students, who frequently use Google and Wikipedia to support their learning. She adds, 'students approach their studies the same way they organize their lives: through a formula based on interest, priority and return on investment' and hence, 'students aren't just seekers of knowledge but also seekers of efficiency' (p. 89). This argument is reinforced by Henderson et al. (2015), whose survey shows students making more use of Wikipedia as their studies advance; one possible explanation, from a Disruptive Innovation perspective, is the pursuit of the efficient use of time and resources to accomplish educational goals. The principles of Disruptive Innovation are woven into everyday practice to support learning and teaching.

SOCIAL MEDIA TECHNOLOGIES

Timmis (2012) argues that students have a wealth of digital technologies available to them, but it is unclear whether this is an asset or a burden (p. 4). An alternative to multitasking with technologies is demarcation, and it is more likely that students use specific technologies for specific purposes. Rienties et al. (2013) argue, 'students are now familiar with the format of communication through social learning tools (for example, Facebook, Twitter) and expect these to be replicated in the classroom' (p. 122), but demarcation, this book argues, is a more common practice, with students and lecturers not tending to use social media technologies to support learning and teaching. Hence, a number of interviewees for Timmis's (2012) research employed a demarcation between technologies for study and technologies for social life (pp. 9–10).

Social media technologies are popular, free, convenient and easy to use. They therefore appear to have the hallmarks of disruptive technologies, but the actual picture is more complex. For example, out of the 213 students sampled by Madge et al. (2009), less than 10% were in favour of Facebook being used as a teaching tool. Similarly, Jones et al. (2010) found that, while over 70% of their sample of students drawn from four UK universities had a social media account, they rarely used social media for educational purposes. Irwin et al. (2012), in an Australian context, created a Facebook page for a course but found only around half of the students stated it was effective and, moreover, students' use of Facebook was similar to the use of a VLE, such as catching up on class content (p. 1227). In the USA, Camus et al. (2016) undertook a comparative study of student posts on Facebook and on a VLE and found that the former was better suited to student participation and encouraging peer-to-peer dialogue, but the latter was better, 'for encouraging students to develop coherent arguments and apply course content in other contexts' (p. 84). The medium itself appeared to be a significant determinant of the practice undertaken by users.

The limited adoption of Facebook and other social media technologies in practice to support learning and teaching in higher education supports the argument that students and lecturers practise demarcation; an interviewee of Salmon et al. (2015) described using Facebook to support a course a 'a little too intimate' (p. 10) and an interviewee in my own research stated, 'Adding too many technologies to support teaching/learning, especially where one or two can do the job well, can overwhelm the student (and the educator!)' (Flavin 2012). Moreover, Wang et al. (2012) studied the use of

Facebook as a teaching tool, finding that students preferred it for social networking than for formal learning. In addition, Jones (2012) notes the distracting effect of social media technologies, whose automated processes (such as notifications) can pop up when students or lecturers are working (p. 34), and Junco and Cotten (2012) found that students who used Facebook and texted while doing academic work got poorer results than students who were not similarly distracted or multitasking (their study of 1839 college students in the USA also found that students spent an average of 1 hour and 41 minutes on Facebook). It may well be easier and more convenient for users to have separate technologies supporting their learning and their social lives, which does not mean that Facebook and similar technologies are not used to support learning and teaching, but that social media technologies are likely to occupy a niche in support and are less likely to comprise a front-end platform (Flavin 2016b).

MOOCs

The MOOC is a means by which widening participation in higher education can be achieved, but the position of MOOCs is more complex than it appears at first; MOOCs are free and they are convenient, but they may only be simple and easy to use for people with prior experience of higher education. Hence, MOOCs are not a disruptive technology (this issue is explored in greater depth in Chap. 5), although the FutureLearn platform does follow Christensen's recommendations, comprising a separate, autonomous unit for developing MOOC courses within and beyond the wider institution.

The openness of MOOCs can, in itself, be a problem, as they are open to students to whom they might not be suitable, but a MOOC launched by FutureLearn and reported on by Liyanagunawardena et al. (2015) responded to the problem by communicating clearly the intended audience for an introductory course to computer programming. The openness of the MOOC is thus compromised, but it is a question of the technology attaining a fruitful purpose, of identifying the job to be done (Christensen and Raynor 2003). The MOOC has the potential to be disruptive but, at present, its purpose is too amorphous for the disruption to be realized. The core question of each individual MOOC's purpose needs to be clarified, beyond aims and objectives and into a clear sense of why the course exists. In the absence of a clear job-to-be-done, the MOOC is not a disruptive innovation but, instead, another form of an online course, a mode of learning which has been available since the 1990s (Lawton and Katsomitros 2012). The MOOC is a sustaining innovation.

BRING YOUR OWN DEVICE

A significant development in technology enhanced learning is the emergence of Bring Your Own Device (BYOD), whereby students use their own devices (typically smartphones or tablet computers) to support their learning. BYOD comprises a disruptive innovation because it is convenient; students and lecturers can access resources at any time. Moreover, as the technology is owned by the user, they will, after a brief time, find it easy to use. In addition, BYOD is an increasingly affordable technology practice. The New Media Consortium's Horizon Report (Johnson et al. 2016) in the USA argues, 'the question is no longer whether to allow them in the classroom, but how to most effectively integrate and support them' (p. 36). The report also notes the spread of BYOD in higher education and argues that BYOD can reduce overall technology spending, as the cost of the hardware is shifted from the institution to the individual, an argument also made by Sanders (2011, p. 67). The growth of BYOD is also evident in a study by Henderson et al. (2015) of 1658 students at two Australian universities, which shows around 40% of students making no use of computers provided by the university (though this also means a majority of the students are making at least some use of university hardware).

Notwithstanding the convenience and ease of use of BYOD, the approach does involve the transfer of costs from the institution to the individual, and in this sense BYOD is symptomatic of wider trends in higher education in many countries. That said, a core characteristic of disruptive technologies is that they are cheap, which means the user can manage the burden of costs; a JISC (2011) report in the UK claims, 'The low cost of ownership means that some students can afford newer-specification devices than colleges and universities can supply' (p. 7). However, if some students cannot afford smartphones or similar technologies, they are at risk of digital exclusion.

Nagy et al. (2016), in a revised definition of Disruptive Innovation, stress the importance of ownership. The fact of ownership in relation to technology enhanced learning is significant because ownership of the technology lessens the university's mediation between the student or lecturer and knowledge resources. Students and lecturers have their own technologies to access, quickly and conveniently, resources over which the university has no control, other than its provision of a wi-fi network. However, the absence of a pedagogical model for BYOD can lead to smartphones and similar devices comprising a distraction for students, as was found in a study conducted by Tossell et al. (2015): 'Smartphones support ubiquitous informal learning opportunities, but the educational model being used currently provides limited need for this beneficial activity' (p. 722). Pedagogy has yet to catch up with practice, but this is typical of Disruptive Innovation.

Learning Analytics

A potential benefit of technology enhanced learning is learning analytics, a process which gathers details of students' actions in online environments in order to 'transform the data gathered in actionable information' (Conde and Hernandez-Garcia 2015, p. 1). The Association for Learning Technology's review for 2015 identified data and analytics as having the biggest jump in perceived importance for technology enhanced learning in the UK higher education sector (p. 4). The aims of learning analytics can include the identification of at-risk students and the gathering of data to effect real-time or just-in-time improvements in learning and teaching. A more personalized form of learning may thus emerge from the tracking of each learner's progress. A case study at Purdue University in the USA (Arnold and Pistilli 2012) measured students' engagement with the university's VLE, aligning it with a traffic light system to identify students who were not engaging with the system. Moreover, and rather than seeing this approach as invasive, students at Purdue appreciated it (p. 269).

Siemens and Baker (2012) argue that large data sets are available for technology enhanced learning and that areas other than higher education have used data to develop their provision: 'In sectors such as government, health care, and industry, data mining and analytics have become increasingly prominent for gaining insight into organizational activities. Drawing value from data in order to guide planning, interventions, and decision-making is an important and fundamental shift in how education systems function.' Furthermore, Facebook, Twitter, YouTube, LinkedIn and Google Plus all have facilities for gathering data on users' interactions with the system (King 2015); the use of analytics thus has commercial as well as educational implications, as stated by Burd et al. (2015) who argue analytics can be used in higher education to identify markets in which to target advertising campaigns (p. 42).

The educational and commercial potential of analytics is considerable, but there are also problems relating to privacy and the safety of student data (Johnson et al. 2016, p. 39). Moreover, there are limits to the value of the data, because, for example, it records visits undertaken to a VLE but not the quality of learning undertaken on the VLE, a problem recognized by Rienties et al. (2016). Furthermore, and as identified by Ferguson et al. (2014), learning analytics needs the engagement of students and lecturers, and of support staff and administrators, and Gašević et al. (2014) argue, 'higher education institutions are not mature data-informed organizations... A predominance of institutions have poorly developed capacity and competencies in learning analytics' (p. 83). Having acknowledged those limitations, the reformulation of technology enhanced learning, from providing resources or interaction to providing analysis to determine future delivery, is a radical one, with implications for programme content and student support.

Baer and Campbell (2012) see analytics as both a sustaining and disruptive innovation; a sustaining innovation in the sense that analytics can identify at-risk students, but a disruptive innovation because analytics could be used, 'to power adaptive systems that adapt to the learner's needs based on behaviours of the individual as well as of past students' patterns' (p. 62), thus creating more personalized forms of learning. Sharples et al. (2015) build on learning analytics to identify 'adaptive teaching' (p. 5), whereby data about a learner's online practice can be used to personalize learning; they also identify 'stealth assessment' (p. 5), with data on learners' usage of online environments enabling ongoing monitoring of their progress. However, Sharples et al. (2015) also note: 'Concerns have been raised about collection of vast amounts of data and the ethics of using computers to monitor a person's every action' (p. 5). Setting ethics to one side, there remains a core challenge of using learning analytics effectively and developing practical strategies to enable its implementation, but there is also a significant incentive to personalize learning, an outcome with the potential to enhance the student experience in higher education.

Learning analytics is a disruptive innovation because it provides convenient and free data. Its ease of use is less clear cut, as strategies will need to be devised to gather and analyse the data, but learning analytics is disruptive because of how it can truncate the gap between gathering and analyzing data, and applying strategies. From identifying at-risk students to creating individual learning pathways, learning analytics can enhance learning, teaching, assessment and support (Flavin 2016b).

CONCLUSION

Christensen's work is important for this book because it enables the identification of disruptive technologies and shows how disruption emerges
through practice. Furthermore, Christensen's work identifies the typical
criteria of disruptive technologies (cheaper, simpler, smaller, more convenient (1997, p. xv)), leading to what Mukunda (2010) calls 'pattern recognition' for Disruptive Innovation (p. 214), with Disruptive Innovation
subsequently reshaping the pattern of preferences in a market (Henderson
2006, p. 9). Consequently, this book examines technologies conforming to
Christensen's criteria in order to explore their impact on learning and
teaching in higher education.

Disruptive Innovation is also a valuable approach because it emphasizes
practice rather than design and is thus rooted in actual practices with
technologies to support learning and teaching. Furthermore, Disruptive
Innovation suggests technologies take hold not by confronting existing
technologies but by building their own networks of users. This book is
therefore focused on how and why students and lecturers use disruptive
technologies in preference to sustaining technologies. By looking at specific
disruptive technologies, this book enables an understanding of how universities can engage with disruptive technologies in practice.

In a discussion of the higher education system in the USA, Crow and
Debars (2015) identify a problem, namely, that tradition weighs heavily and
therefore anything that deviates from tradition is disruptive (p. 121). Consequently, universities are prone to structural inertia, which does not prohibit change but tends to favour incremental over disruptive change
(p. 125). Christensen and Eyring (2011) argue that an absence of disruptive
technologies is one of the reasons for a lack of disruption in higher education (p. 18) and Christensen et al. (2015) underline the point when they
argue that the relative standing of universities in the USA remains largely
unchanged. In a similar vein, de Langen and van den Bosch (2013) argue,
'teachers deliver lectures in the same way as their predecessors did for
centuries' (p. 216). This cultural trait extends beyond universities:
Christensen and Raynor (2003) argue, 'Middle managers typically hesitate
to throw their weight behind new product concepts whose market is not
assured' (p. 10), middle managers being, in Christensen and Raynor's
argument, a key constituency in determining which innovative ideas
are taken forward, thus illustrating the problem identified by Bower
and Christensen (1995) concerning institutional reluctance to take risks.

Yu and Hang (2009) argue that structural features of organizations militate against disruption by encouraging middle managers to defend their existing territory and practices rather than innovate; disruptive innovation can be suppressed in the face of established, even entrenched, practices. Furthermore, Christensen et al. (2008) argue 'organizations cannot *naturally* disrupt themselves' (p. 75, emphasis in original). Back in higher education, Crow and Debars (2015) argue that structural inertia is inappropriate 'for institutions dedicated to the production of knowledge and diffusion of innovation' (p. 125). They further argue, 'An appreciation of the role of technological innovation in our knowledge-based society requires less restrictive definitions of both *technology* and *innovation*' (p. 155, emphasis in original). The innovative use of technology in universities, therefore, is not a given, but a challenge.

Crow and Debars (2015) argue for the need for universities to create 'an ecosystem of innovation' (p. 190). DaSilva et al. (2013) take a less organic, more deliberate standpoint when they argue, 'A viable model is crucial for the successful commercialisation of disruptive technologies' (p. 1161); they further argue that institutions are not disrupted by technologies per se, but by their own inability to change their business model (p. 1168). The application of technology enhanced learning in higher education has tended to involve the contortion of the technology to serve the existing pedagogical model, shaped by the underpinning historical pressures suggested by Crow and Debars (2015), but users create disruption from the ground up through their practice, and institutions can nurture an ecosystem of innovation by observing and engaging with the innovation taking place in their midst. Curtailing technology's potential in the interests of a controlled classroom environment sustains an existing pedagogy, but artificially so; a more interesting and relevant approach might be to allow innovative practice, to see where it leads and to understand how technology can reconfigure classroom practice and power relations within classrooms.

In view of the rapidly changing economics of higher education, most noticeably the substantial increase in fees in many countries, there is a possibility that expectations of higher education will alter and that the provision of higher education will diversify. Christensen and Eyring (2011) point out a core fact of higher education in the USA, 'Since the late 1980s, college tuition and fees have risen 440 percent, four times faster than inflation' (p. 202), a phenomenon which, in other circumstances, would look like a bubble. Similarly, de Langen and van den Bosch (2013) point out that higher education costs in the USA are rising 10% each year

(p. 216), and Behara and Davis (2015) state that tuition fees in higher education in the USA are second only to the rising cost of health care (p. 312). Tuition fees are also rising in the UK. Universities therefore need to find new ways of working with the technologies with which learners and teachers interact on a daily basis, both to justify cost and to enhance the learning experience. The structural inertia identified by Crow and Debars (2015) comprises a roadblock to change. The university has shown itself to be a durable model, but economic change can spark tangible changes to practice.

This chapter has summarized Christensen's work on disruptive technologies and Disruptive Innovation and has looked at how subsequent researchers have built upon and challenged the original theory. The chapter has also explored the applicability of the category of disruptive technology and the theory of Disruptive Innovation to technology enhanced learning. In addition, the chapter has considered specific technologies and specific practices. The chapter argues that purposes for technologies are created through practice and that Christensen's core criteria (1997, p. xv) comprise a useful means of evaluating technologies and their likely success in higher education.

The next chapter takes disruptive technologies and analyses their impact on higher education through the lens of Activity Theory (Leontiev 1978, 1981; Vygotsky 1927, 1930) and expansive learning (Engeström 1987, 2001), focusing on social factors in technology enhanced learning. Thereafter, in Chap. 4, the book examines the Community of Practice theory to better understand how disruptive technology enhanced learning influences learning communities and to better understand where and how Disruptive Innovation occurs. By these means, the book aims to understand how disruptive technologies are consequential and impactful and how the use of technologies in universities is conditioned by wider contexts: economic, historical and social.

REFERENCES

Arnold, K. E., & Pistilli, M. D. (2012). Course signals at Purdue: Using learning analytics to increase student success. In *LAK 12: Proceedings of the 2nd international conference on learning analytics and knowledge* (pp. 267–270). New York: ACM.

Baer, L., & Campbell, J. (2012). From metrics to analytics, reporting to action: Analytics' role in changing the learning environment. In D. G. Oblinger (Ed.), *Game changers: Education and information technologies*. Louisville: Educause.

Bagozzi, R. P. (2007). The legacy of the technology acceptance model and a proposal for a paradigm shift. *Journal of the Association for Information Systems, 8*(4), 244–254.

Behara, R. S., & Davis, M. M. (2015). Navigating disruptive innovation in undergraduate business education. *Journal of Innovative Education, 13*(3), 305–326.

Bennett, D. (2014, June 21). Clayton Christensen responds to *New Yorker* takedown of "Disruptive Innovation". *Bloomberg Business.* Retrieved from http://www.bloomberg.com/bw/articles/2014-06-20/clayton-christensen-responds-to-new-yorker-takedown-of-disruptive-innovation

Blin, F., & Munro, M. (2008). Why hasn't technology disrupted academics' teaching practices? Understanding resistance to change through the lens of activity theory. *Computers and Education, 50,* 475–490.

Bower, J. L., & Christensen, C. M. (1995). Disruptive technologies: Catching the wave. *Harvard Business Review, 1*(13), 43–53.

Burd, E. L., Smith, S. P., & Reisman, S. (2015). Exploring business models for MOOCs in higher education. *Innovative Higher Education, 40,* 37–49.

Camus, M., Hurt, N. E., Larson, L. R., & Prevost, L. (2016). Facebook as an online teaching tool: Effects on student participation, learning, and overall course performance. *College Teaching, 64*(2), 84–94.

Chena, C., Zhang, J., & Guoc, R.-S. (2016). The D-Day, V-Day, and bleak days of a disruptive technology: A new model for ex-ante evaluation of the timing of technology disruption. *European Journal of Operational Research, 251,* 562–574.

Christensen, C. M. (1997). *The innovator's dilemma: When new technologies cause great firms to fail.* Boston: Harvard Business School Press.

Christensen, C. M. (2006). The ongoing process of building a theory of disruption. *The Journal of Product Innovation Management, 23,* 39–55.

Christensen, C. M., & Eyring, H. J. (2011). *The innovative university: Changing the DNA of higher education from the inside out.* San Francisco: Jossey-Bass.

Christensen, C. M., & Raynor, M. E. (2003). *The innovator's solution: Creating and sustaining successful growth.* Boston: Harvard Business School Press.

Christensen, C. M., Horn, M. B., & Johnson, C. W. (2008). *Disrupting class: How disruptive innovation will change the way the world learns.* New York: McGraw-Hill.

Christensen, C.M., Horn, M.B., Caldera, L., & Soares, L. (2011). *Disrupting college: How disruptive innovation can deliver quality and affordability to postsecondary education.* Mountain View: Center for American Progress and Innosight Institute. Retrieved from https://cdn.americanprogress.org/wp-content/uploads/issues/2011/02/pdf/disrupting_college_execsumm.pdf

Christensen, C. M., Raynor, M. E., & McDonald, R. (2015). What is disruptive innovation? *Harvard Business Review, 93*(12), 44–53.

Christensen, C. M., Bartman, T., & van Bever, D. (2016, Fall). The hard truth about business model innovation. *MIT Sloan Management Review.* Retrieved from http://sloanreview.mit.edu/article/the-hard-truth-about-business-model-innovation/

Conde, M. A., & Hernandez-Garcia, A. (2015). Learning analytics for educational decision making. *Computers in Human Behavior, 47,* 1–3.

Cortez, N. (2014). Regulating disruptive innovation. *Berkeley Technology Law Journal, 29*(1), 175–228.

Crow, M. M., & Dabars, W. B. (2015). *Designing the new American University.* Baltimore: John Hopkins University Press.

Cuban, L. (2001). *Oversold and underused: Computers in the classroom.* Cambridge, MA: Harvard University Press.

Danneels, E. (2004). Disruptive technology reconsidered: A critique and research agenda. *The Journal of Product Information Management, 21,* 246–258.

Danneels, E. (2006). From the guest editor: Dialogue on the effects of disruptive technology on firms and industries. *The Journal of Product Information Management, 23,* 2–4.

DaSilva, C. M., Trkman, P., Desouza, K., & Lindič, J. (2013). Disruptive technologies: A business model perspective on cloud computing. *Technology Analysis and Strategic Management, 25*(10), 1161–1173.

Davis, F. D. (1989). Perceived usefulness, perceived ease of use, and user acceptance of information technology. *MIS Quarterly, 13*(3), 319–340.

De Langen, F., & van den Bosch, H. (2013). Massive open online courses: Disruptive innovations or disturbing inventions? *Open Learning: The Journal of Open, Distance and e-Learning, 28*(3), 216–226.

Denning, S. (2016). Christensen updates disruption theory. *Strategy and Leadership, 44*(2), 10–16.

Edmunds, R., Thorpe, M., & Conole, G. (2012). Student attitudes and use of ICT in course study, work and social activity: A technology acceptance model approach. *British Journal of Educational Technology, 43*(1), 71–84.

Engeström, Y. (1987). *Learning by expanding: An activity-theoretical approach to developmental research.* Helsinki: Orienta-Konsultit Oy. Retrieved from http://lchc.ucsd.edu/MCA/Paper/Engestrom/expanding/toc.htm

Engeström, Y. (2001). Expansive learning at work: Toward an activity theoretical reconceptualization. *Journal of Education and Work, 14*(1), 133–156.

Ferguson, R., Clow, D., Macfadyen, L., Essa, A., Dawson, S., & Alexander, S. (2014). Setting learning analytics in context: Overcoming the barriers to large-scale adoption. *LAK14: Proceedings of the fourth international conference on learning analytics and knowledge* (pp. 251–253). http://dl.acm.org/citation.cfm?id=2567592

Flavin, M. (2012). Disruptive technologies in higher education. *Research in Learning Technology, 20,* 102–111.

Flavin, M. (2015). Home and away: The use of institutional and non-institutional technologies to support learning and teaching. *Interactive Learning Environments*. doi: 10.1080/10494820.2015.1041404

Flavin, M. (2016a). Disruptive conduct: The impact of disruptive technologies on social relations in higher education. *Innovations in Education and Teaching International, 15*(1), 3–15.

Flavin, M. (2016b). Technology-enhanced learning and higher education. *Oxford Review of Economic Policy, 32*(4), 632–645.

Gašević, D., Dawson, S., Rogers, T., & Gasevic, D. (2014). Learning analytics should not promote one size fits all: The effects of instructional conditions in predicting academic success. *Internet and Higher Education, 28*, 68–84.

Govindarajan, V., & Kopalle, P. (2006). The usefulness of measuring disruptiveness of innovations ex post in making ex ante predictions. *The Journal of Product Innovation Management, 23*(1), 12–18.

Govindarajan, G., Kopalle, P. K., & Danneels, E. (2011). The effects of mainstream and emerging customer orientations on radical and disruptive innovations. *The Journal of Product Innovation Management, 28*(1), 121–132.

Hart, S. L., & Christensen, C. M. (2002). The great leap: Driving innovation from the base of the Pyramid. *MIT Sloan Management Review, 44*(1), 51–56.

Henderson, R. (2006). The innovator's dilemma as a problem of organisational competence. *The Journal of Product Innovation Management, 23*, 5–11.

Henderson, M., Selwyn, N., & Aston, R. (2015). What works and why? Student perceptions of "useful" digital technology in university teaching and learning. *Studies in Higher Education*. doi:10.1080/03075079.2015.1007946.

Hillis, K., Petit, M., & Jarrett, K. (2013). *Google and the culture of search*. Abingdon: Routledge.

Irwin, C., Ball, L., Desbrow, B., & Leveritt, M. (2012). Students' perceptions of using Facebook as an interactive learning resource at university. *Australasian Journal of Educational Technology, 28*(7), 1221–1232.

Jisc. (2011). *Emerging practice in a digital age: A guide to technology-enhanced institutional innovation*. Bristol: Jisc.

Johnson, L., Adams-Becker, S., Cummins, M., Estrada, V., Freeman, A., & Hall, C. (2016). *NMC horizon report: 2016 higher education edition*. Austin: The New Media Consortium.

Jones, C. (2012). Networked learning, stepping beyond the net generation and digital natives. In L. Dirckinck-Holmfeld, V. Hodgson, & D. Mc Connell (Eds.), *Exploring the theory, pedagogy and practice of networked learning* (pp. 27–41). New York: Springer.

Jones, N., Blackley, H., Fitzgibbon, K., & Chew, E. (2010). Get out of MySpace! *Computers and Education, 54*(3), 776–782.

Junco, R., & Cotten, S. R. (2012). No A 4 U: The relationship between multitasking and academic performance. *Computers and Education, 59*, 505–514.

Karlsson, N. (2014). The crossroads of academic electronic availability: How well does Google Scholar measure up against a university-based metadata system in 2014? *Current Science, 10*, 1661–1665.

King, D. L. (2015). Analytics, goals, and strategy for social media. *Library Technology Reports, 51*(1), 26–32.

Laurillard, D. (2013). Foreword to the second edition. In H. Beetham & R. Sharpe (Eds.), *Rethinking pedagogy for a digital age* (2nd ed.). Abingdon: Routledge.

Lawrence, K. (2015). Today's college students: Skimmers, scanners and efficiency-seekers. *Information Services and Use, 35*, 89–93.

Lawton, W., & Katsomitros, A. (2012). *MOOCs and disruptive innovation: The challenge to HE business models.* The Observatory on Borderless Higher Education. Retrieved from http://www.obhe.ac.uk/documents/view_details?id=929

Lawton, W., Ahmed, M., Angulo, T., Axel-Berg, A., Burrows, A., & Katsomitros, A. (2013). Horizon scanning: What will higher education look like in 2020? The observatory on borderless higher education. http://www.obhe.ac.uk/documents/view_details?id=934

Leontiev, A. N. (1978). *Activity, consciousness and personality* (trans. Hall, M.J.). Englewood Cliffs: Prentice Hall.

Leontiev, A. N. (1981). *Problems of the development of the mind.* Moscow: Progress.

Lepore, J. (2014). The disruption machine: What the gospel of innovation gets wrong. *The New Yorker, 90*(17), 30–36.

Livingstone, D. (2011). Second life is dead: Long live second life? *Educause Review, 46*(2), 61–62.

Liyanagunawardena, T. R., Lundqvist, K. O., & Williams, S. A. (2015). Who are with us: MOOC learners on a FutureLearn course. *British Journal of Educational Technology, 46*(3), 557–569.

Lorange, P., & Rembiszewski, J. (2016). Customer related innovations in the 21st century. *Organizational Dynamics, 45*(2), 147–153.

Madge, C., Meek, J., Wellens, J., & Hooley, T. (2009). Facebook, social integration and informal learning at university: It is more for socialising and talking to friends about work than for actually doing work. *Learning, Media and Technology, 34*(2), 141–155.

Mahenge, M. P. J., & Sanga, C. (2016). ICT for e-learning in three higher education institutions in Tanzania. *Knowledge Management and E-Learning: An International Journal, 8*(1), 200–212.

Markides, C. (2006). Disruptive innovation; in need of better theory. *The Journal of Product Innovation Management, 23*, 19–25.

Markides, C. (2008). *Game-changing strategies: How to create new market space in established industries by breaking the rules.* San Francisco: Jossey-Bass.

McGregor, J. (2007). *Clayton Christensen's innovation brain.* Bloomberg. Retrieved from http://www.bloomberg.com/news/articles/2007-06-15/

clayton-christensens-innovation-brainbusinessweek-business-news-stock-market-and-financial-advice

Moore, G. (2004). Darwin and the demon. *Harvard Business Review, 82*(7–8), 86–92.

Mukunda, G. (2010). We cannot go on: Disruptive innovation and the First World War Royal Navy. *Security Studies, 19*, 124–159.

Nagy, D., Schussler, J., & Dubinsky, A. (2016). Defining and identifying disruptive innovations. *Industrial Marketing Management, 57*, 119–126.

Naughton, J. (2012). *From Gutenberg to Zuckerberg: What you really need to know about the internet*. London: Quercus.

Ng'ambi, D. (2013). Effective and ineffective uses of emerging technologies: Towards a transformative pedagogical model. *British Journal of Educational Technology, 44*(4), 652–661.

Organisation for Economic Co-operation and Development, Centre for Educational Research and Innovation. (2009). *New millennium learners in higher education: Evidence and Policy Implications*. Paris: OECD, CERI.

Pisano, G. P. (2015). You need an innovation strategy. *Harvard Business Review, 93*(6), 3–12.

Rambe, P., & Nel, L. (2015). Technological utopia, dystopia and ambivalence: Teaching with social media at a South African university. *British Journal of Educational Technology, 46*(3), 629–648.

Reinsmith-Jones, K., Kibbe, S., Crayton, T., & Campbell, E. (2015). Use of second life in social work education: Virtual world experiences and their effect on students. *Journal of Social Work Education, 51*, 90–108.

Rienties, B., Brouwer, N., & Lygo-Baker, S. (2013). The effects of online professional development on teachers' beliefs and intentions towards learning facilitation and technology. *Teaching and Teacher Education, 29*, 122–131.

Rienties, B., Boroowa, A., Cross, S., Kubiak, C., Mayles, K., & Murphy, S. (2016). Analytics4Action evaluation framework: A review of evidence-based learning analytics interventions at the Open University UK. *Journal of Interactive Media in Education, 1*(2), 1–11.

Robotham, D. (2012). Student part-time employment: Characteristics and consequences. *Education and Training, 54*(1), 65–75.

Salmon, G., Ross, B., Pechenkina, E., & Chase, A. M. (2015). The space for social media in structured online learning. *Research in Learning Technology, 23*, 1–14.

Sanders, J. (2011). The challenge of cost-effective technology enhanced learning for medical education. *Education for Primary Care, 22*, 66–69.

Selwyn, N., & Gorard, S. (2016). Students' use of Wikipedia as an academic resource – Patterns of use and patterns of usefulness. *Internet and Higher Education, 28*, 28–34.

Sharples, M., Adams, A., Alozie, N., Ferguson, R., Fitzgerald, E., Gaved, M., McAndrew, P., Means, B., Remold, J., Rienties, B., Roschelle, J., Vogt, K.,

Whitelock, D., & Yarnall, L. (2015). *Innovating pedagogy 2015*. Milton Keynes: Open University.

Siemens, G., & Baker, R. S. J. (2012). Learning analytics and educational data mining: Towards communication and collaboration. *LAK '12: Proceedings of the 2nd International Conference on Learning Analytics and Knowledge*, Vancouver, 29 April–2 May, pp. 252–254.

Skarzynski, P., & Rufat-Latre, J. (2011). Lesson to jumpstart disruptive innovation. *Strategy and Leadership, 39*(1), 5–10.

Smagorinsky, P. (2001). If meaning is constructed, what is it made from?: Toward a cultural theory of reading author(s). *Review of Educational Research, 71*(1), 133–169.

Sodexo. (2016). *The Sodexo University lifestyle survey*. London: Sodexo.

Timmis, S. (2012). Constant companions: Instant messaging conversations as sustainable supportive study structures amongst undergraduate peers. *Computers and Education, 59*, 3–18.

Tossell, C. C., Kortum, P., Shephard, C., & Zhong, L. (2015). You can lead a horse to water but you cannot make him learn: Smartphone use in higher education. *British Journal of Educational Technology, 46*(4), 713–724.

Tripsas, M., & Gavetti, G. (2000). Capabilities, cognition, and inertia: Evidence from digital imaging. *Strategic Management Journal, 21*(10/11), 1147–1161.

Tseng, H. W., Tang, Y., & Morris, B. (2016). Evaluation of iTunes University courses through instructional design strategies and m-learning framework. *Educational Technology and Society, 19*(1), 199–210.

Vygotsky, L. (1930). The socialist alteration of man. In R. Van Der Veet & J. Valsiner (Eds.), *The Vygotsky reader* (pp. 175–184). Oxford: Blackwell.

Wang, Q., Woo, H. L., Quek, C. L., Yang, Y., & Liu, M. (2012). Using the Facebook group as a learning management system: An exploratory study. *British Journal of Educational Technology, 43*(3), 428–438.

Wenger, E. (1998). *Communities of practice: Learning, meaning, and identity*. Cambridge: Cambridge University Press.

Yamagata-Lynch, L. C., Cowan, J., & Luetkehans, L. M. (2015). Transforming disruptive technology into sustainable technology: Understanding the front-end design of an online program at a brick-and-mortar university. *Internet and Higher Education, 26*, 1–18.

Yu, D., & Hang, C. C. (2009). A reflective review of disruptive innovation theory. *International Journal of Management Reviews, 12*(4), 435–452.

Zold, E. (2014). Virtual travel in second life. *Pedagogy: Critical Approaches to Teaching Literature, Language, Composition and Culture, 14*(2), 225–250.

CHAPTER 3

'Why Can't I Just Google It?' What Disruptive Innovation Means for Higher Education

INTRODUCTION

The previous chapter examined disruptive technologies and the theory of Disruptive Innovation in order to identify technologies and practices with the potential to disrupt learning and teaching in higher education. This chapter builds on the previous chapter by incorporating a technique for analysing disruptive technology use in higher education. Having used Christensen's work in the previous chapter to identify disruptive technologies, this chapter introduces a framework which is used to analyse the impact of disruptive technologies on higher education and anticipates the subject of Chap. 4 by considering how the use of disruptive technologies influences higher education communities.

Activity Theory (Leontiev 1978, 1981), also known as Cultural-Historical Activity Theory, is a framework for analysing purposeful human activity; it is rooted in work on psychology undertaken by Vygotsky in the Soviet Union in the 1920s. In Activity Theory, individual human subjects are not static and inviolable entities but are constructed and reconstructed through their interactions with their environments. Moreover, the environments themselves are subject to change. This book is interested in the interaction between individual human subjects and their environments and in what the interaction implies for the use of disruptive and sustaining technologies to support learning and teaching in higher education. The use of technologies responds to or produces purposes, but use does not occur in

© The Author(s) 2017   53
M. Flavin, *Disruptive Technology Enhanced Learning*,
DOI 10.1057/978-1-137-57284-4_3

a vacuum. Indeed, the contexts for the activity are saturated historically and socially.

Activity Theory argues that purposeful human actions are mediated through the use of tools. Bennett (2010) argues that Activity Theory is a useful analytical lens because, 'it moves the focus of analysis from the technological tool to the way that tool is used by people to achieve a purpose' (p. 10), eschewing technological determinism and focusing instead on practice (and, incidentally, linking Activity Theory with Disruptive Innovation as defined by Christensen and Raynor (2003)). Consequently, the primary unit of analysis when investigating human activity via Activity Theory is human activity itself.

The chapter examines Activity Theory chronologically, starting with Vygotsky, noting the theory's development and focusing on its recent interpretations and analyses. The first generation of Activity Theory, associated with Vygotsky and Leontiev, adopts a triadic model. The second, associated with Engeström, adds social elements to the original model, focuses on adult learning and introduces the theory of expansive learning. Third-generation Activity Theory looks beyond this book's core area of enquiry; Engeström and Glăveanu (2012) argue, 'third generation activity theory... expand[s] the unit of analysis from a single activity system to multiple, minimally two, interacting activity systems' (p. 516). Spinuzzi (2014) argues that fourth generation Activity Theory is characterized by 'boundary crossing ... in temporary collaborations across networks of interrelated activities' (p. 91), exploring relationships and tensions across multiple activity systems. This book is weighted towards second generation Activity Theory in practice, in order to focus on how social factors address and illuminate the specific question of technology usage in individual and institutional contexts, though it is also interested in boundary crossing as a means of producing innovation in communities.

The chapter also considers the importance of contradictions in technology enhanced learning in higher education and examines how disruptive technologies exemplify new technology enhanced learning practices and their implications. Contradiction in an activity system is a multi-layered process rooted in the accumulation of tensions over time, and activity systems are not static but are always in some stage of development; Czerniewicz et al. (2016) argue, 'an examination of contradictions can help to understand how innovation occurs' (p. 290). Similarly, Roth (2004) argues, 'the very notion of activity... at the heart of Engeström's representation embodies change' (p. 3). The focus on second generation

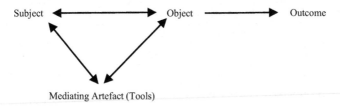

Fig. 3.1 First-generation activity system (After Vygotsky 1978, p. 40)

Activity Theory in this book leads to the introduction of the concept of expansive learning, which is also examined in relation to disruptive technology enhanced learning. The chapter also discusses the role of tools in Activity Theory and features Wikipedia as a case study.

VYGOTSKY

Vygotsky's *Mind in Society* (1978), while focused on the development of children with particular reference to the acquisition of language, has wider relevance, especially in relation to how humans use tools, both physical and abstract, to accomplish tasks.

Vygotsky conceptualized the original model of human activity as a triangle (Fig. 3.1).

Vygotsky's model shows how human beings (subjects) use physical tools and abstract resources as mediators, in pursuit of objects (purposes), leading to the production of outcomes. The object in an activity system is a particularly important node: Jonassen and Rohrer-Murphy (1999) argue that the object in Activity Theory 'represents the intention that motivates the activity' (p. 63), while Foot (2014) argues, 'understanding an activity system requires understanding its object' (p. 333). The object comprises the activity's purpose, and understanding the purpose is necessary to understand the activity system.

To illustrate what is meant by physical tools and abstract resources, a person (subject) wanting to put a nail into a wall (object) will use a hammer (tool) for the purpose. However, a student using an acronym for the object of remembering facts for an exam is also using the acronym as a tool, albeit that the tool is a sign: 'The sign acts as an instrument of psychological activity in a manner analogous to the role of a tool in labor' (Vygotsky 1978, p. 52). Tool and sign are not conflated in Activity Theory, a point repeated by Leontiev (see Rückriem 2010, p. 31), but the close, analogous relationship allows both physical tool and abstract resource to be interpreted as the mediating artefact in an activity system.

According to Smagorinsky (2009), the primary tool for humans is speech (p. 89), and hence tools are used to mediate object-driven activity in daily life. Furthermore, the design of tools reflects the cultures within which the tools are produced, as Foot (2014) notes: 'in a culture ... in which moving dirt manually is essential to survival and men do the work of shovelling, the typical length of shovel handles will correspond to the average height of adult males in that culture' (p. 331). Tools are both quotidian and culturally specific.

One of Vygotsky's major achievements was, according to Engeström (2015), to forge a new relationship between subject and object by positing 'an intermediate link between the stimulus and the response' (p. 47). Vygotsky (1978) himself had argued, 'Every elementary form of behaviour presupposes a *direct* reaction to the task set before the organism ... But the structure of sign operations requires an intermediate link between the stimulus and the response. This intermediate link is a second order stimulus (sign) that is drawn into the operation where it fulfils a special function' (p. 39, emphasis in original). This idea of mediation is central to Vygotsky's ideas (the seemingly natural relationship between subject and object is disrupted), as is the idea that the mediating influence can affect the subject as well as the object. The movement in an activity system is not in one direction only; the subject (the individual or group undertaking the task) is also subject to change.

THE SUBJECT IN ACTIVITY THEORY

In 'The Socialist Alteration of Man' (1930), Vygotsky challenges the dualism between the individual and the social. Instead of seeing the individual as unique and inviolable, Vygotsky argues that identity is constructed ultimately by economic forces of production and resultant social relations: 'We have to proceed from the basic assumption that intellectual production is determined by the form of material production' (p. 177). More broadly, Bakhurst (2009) has identified a core tenet of Activity Theory, 'that the very nature and possibility of our minds depends in some deep sense on our membership in a community' (p. 197). In addition, Engeström and Miettenen (1999) argue, 'Human nature is not found within the human individual but in the movement between the inside and outside' (p. 5), Jonassen and Rohrer-Murphy (1999) argue, 'consciousness is the result of everyday practice' (p. 64), while Miettenen (1999) states, 'consciousness does not exist situated inside the head of the individual' (p. 173). Essentialist perspectives on identity have no place in Activity Theory. If Vygotsky and subsequent writers on Activity Theory are correct, then consciousness, thoughts and their articulation through practice are determined by the material and historical conditions within which any individual subject resides. Vygotsky's position in this regard implies a link to Markides (2006) from a Disruptive Innovation perspective, with the potential uses of a technology, building on Vygotsky's argument, being determined by economic and social forces, starting from the economic limitations of access to technology, through to social limitations of access to technology owned or otherwise paid for by universities, through to the impact of marketing influencing both the selection and usage of technologies.

There is a further connection between Vygotsky and Christensen in the sense that Vygotsky, as argued by Hung and Chen (2001), focuses on both the product and the process of development (p. 4), an approach which is necessarily longitudinal: the same point is also made more recently in relation to Activity Theory by Sannino et al. (2016). As with Disruptive Innovation, development and transformation in Activity Theory is traced over time, and can take a long time.

Vygotsky's core argument that consciousness, subjectivity, is determined by historical and social forces continues to comprise an article of faith in Activity Theory studies (for example, Roth 2007) and is also partly echoed in the Community of Practice theory, which argues that identity is a 'work in progress, shaped by efforts – both individual and collective – to create a coherence through time' (Wenger 1998, p. 45). Practice with technologies is undertaken by subjects who are themselves subject to economic, historical, social and commercial influences and thus do not act in isolation.

Vygotsky (1930) argues that functions of consciousness such as imagination emerge and develop not from an inviolable essence of self but 'in connection with the development of the form of socially defined activity that we call play' (p. 123), though it is worth noting that 'Vygotsky's notion of play refers to experimental activity designed to create possibilities and not to the idea that learning should involve merriment' (Smagorinsky 2009, p. 86). Huizinga (1971/1938) had previously argued that play is an instinct in human beings, which bodes well for a wide range of activities with technologies, including recreational activities. Activity Theory argues that consciousness can change and develop through play and practice. Having readily available technologies with a range of potential uses creates opportunities for play, opportunities which are necessary, in Vygotsky's argument, to develop functions of consciousness such as imagination. Practice with technologies has the potential to change consciousness, not in a direct and linear sense, but in the sense that consciousness is an ongoing work in practice and is influenced by practice.

The idea of learning enabling the development of identity is placed in a more explicitly educational context by Krejsler (2004): 'May we to a larger extent orchestrate the classroom as some sort of agora [an open space] . . . By understanding spaces of learning like that, we would implicitly encourage the student to experiment in ways whereby he/she may eventually acquire for himself/herself more mature autonomy' (p. 501). Vygotsky's (1930) distinctive argument is that play is constructive in a literal, non-value judgement sense, as it constructs functions of consciousness such as imagination. In Activity Theory terms, the interaction of subject, tool and object can shape the subject (the individual user) and thus this book explores how disruptive technology usage impacts on human subjects (individuals) in learning and teaching contexts, as well as arguing that individual subjects' interactions with technology tools, whether the interactions are utilitarian or recreational, are what create purposes for technologies.

Vygotsky (1930) believes in the transformative potential of education: 'It is education which should play the central role in the transformation of man – this road of conscious formation of new generations, the basic form to alter the historical human type' (p. 181). Through education, individuals and groups can question their existing practices, perceive the forces underlying their practices and postulate new practices. Actions create consciousness and thus contain the potential to change and even expand consciousness. Education can create the possibility of a challenge to an existing activity system, as education enables the critical interrogation of economic and social relations.

LEONTIEV

Following Vygotsky's death, his work was taken up by Leontiev, who developed Activity Theory's understanding of collective activity. Engeström (2001) writes, of Vygotsky's work, 'the limitation . . . was that the unit of analysis remained individually focused' (p. 134) and hence part of Leontiev's achievement was to foreground the collaborative and social. Leontiev's (1977, 1981) example of the primeval collective hunt, in which the group undertakes demarcated roles (effectively, a division of labour) for its collective benefit has become an exemplar of Activity Theory, as a community uses its collective resources to achieve an object. Leontiev (1978), following Vygotsky, argues 'the existence of individual mentality, a psyche, in the form of consciousness is impossible' (p. 12), and adds 'consciousness from the very beginning is a social product' (p. 17). He also states, of social interaction, 'it is at this level that human fate is decided' (p. 143). As well as stressing the collaborative aspects of Activity Theory, Leontiev also elaborates on the importance of tools in activity systems, 'Equipment mediates activity connecting man not only with the world of things but also with other people' (p. 59). Leontiev does, however, assert the importance of objects in activity systems: 'It is exactly the object of an activity that gives it a determined direction' (1978, p. 62). Kaptelinin (2005) also argues for the importance of the object in Leontiev's writing, describing it as the 'sense-maker' (p. 5), the object comprising the basis of and motivation for activity. By honing the definition of the nodes in an activity system, Leontiev illuminates Activity Theory and expands its applications. The object is foundational, the subject collective and tools transformational, integrating the subject with the material world and the people in it.

Leontiev (1977, 1981) distinguishes between action and activity. In the context of the hunt the beater who disturbs a hedge to startle the game is undertaking an individual action, whereas the activity is the collective hunt itself (1981, p. 187): 'The frightening of game, for example, in itself is biologically senseless; it acquires sense only in the conditions of collective labour' (1981, p. 189). Engeström et al. (2013) note that Leontiev distinguishes between activity, action and operation; individual actions realise activities, and actions in turn, can be atomized into automatic operations, influenced by the available tools and not normally undertaken consciously by the subject (p. 84). Roth and Lee (2007) argue, 'activities motivate particular action sequences' (p. 201), while Mietennen (1999) argues that operations can be easily transferred to tools, whereas actions requiring imagination also require human interaction (p. 179), an argument which implies that innovation is not a property of tools but a product of human practice. Innovation can occur when human subjects and tools interact in pursuit of objects, or in the construction of a new object. Mietennen (1999) builds on Leontiev but links back to Vygotsky, too, given Vygotsky's stress on the imagination as having the capacity to change and expand consciousness. The use of the imagination is critical in an activity system if innovation is to occur.

SUMMARISING ACTIVITY THEORY

Activity Theory argues subjects' actions are mediated through tools to attain objects. This book traces a similar argument, examining how students and lecturers use tools to get jobs done. From a Technology Acceptance Model perspective, Hu et al. (2003) make a similar argument when they write, 'our analysis suggests a task-centred orientation in teachers' technology evaluation and a pragmatic anchor in their acceptance' (p. 236). The metaphor is interesting because it implies a point of fixity based on use value. The anchor is, in Activity Theory terms, the object, for which purpose tools are applied pragmatically. Furthermore, Activity Theory implies that there are limits to what can be achieved through the interaction of subjects and tools, limits shaped by prevailing economic, historical and social conditions, until individual tensions accrue and produce contradictions, leading to the production of a new activity system with a new object. Activity Theory does not claim fixity, and activity systems are always in some stage of development.

Based on what has been considered thus far, innovation, in the sense of creating something new to meet a need and get a job done is, in Activity Theory, a product of intertraffic requiring a human subject acting imaginatively with tools. The act of innovation implies an absence in an existing activity system because the existing tools (or the way they are used) are not adequate to achieve the object, and in this sense innovation is dialectic, fuelled by tensions creating, over time, a wider contradiction in an existing activity system, potentially producing a new object. Engeström (1993) notes, 'inner contradictions of the activity system can be analysed as the source of disruption, innovation, change, and development of that system, including its individual participants' (p. 65). Activity Theory argues tension is a necessary precondition for innovation.

Theoretical approaches based on the inviolability of individual identity will see innovation as the product of the creative individual, but the approaches adopted in this book view identity as social, with innovation as dialectic, prompted by historical pressures while at the same time posing a challenge to the extant conditions, as new tools are invented or existing tools repurposed, and with the tool, object and subject all influencing each other. Gay et al. (2001) summarize the position by defining Activity Theory as 'draw[ing] attention to the dialectical process by which consciousness, learning, and development simultaneously shape and are shaped by technology' (p. 509). Consciousness, identity, is not fixed, and is therefore, within the terms of this book, an unstable place from which to commence an investigation into the use of technologies. Instead, this book is rooted in practice with technologies, a social activity.

Contradictions, meaning the accumulation of tensions over time, are structural features of activity systems rather than individual manifestations of tension. Contradictions are also necessary to produce substantial progress; Engeström (2015) writes of the, 'production of objectively, societally new activity structures ... out of actions manifesting the inner contradictions of the preceding form of the activity in question' (pp. 98–99), a phenomenon he describes as expansive learning and which will be examined shortly. Furthermore, Engeström (2015) hones his definition of contradictions: 'Contradictions are not the same as problems or conflicts. Contradictions are historically accumulating structural tensions within and between activity systems' (p. 137). Foot (2014) argues, 'Contradictions can be seen as the "places" in an activity system from which innovations emerge ... Rather than ending points, contradictions are starting places' (p. 337), though as they are the product of accumulating tensions, they may be regarded as crux points rather than starting points in the ongoing, finite life of an activity system. Contradictions are problematic but they are also a crucial stage of development, as one activity system is made redundant over time and is replaced by another.

Engeström (1993) notes, 'An activity system always contains sediments of earlier historical modes, as well as buds or shoots of its possible future' (p. 68). Activity Theory breaks purposeful activity down into its component parts and thus facilitates analysis of activity, but the analysis is complicated by the ongoing movement of the system's component parts. There is never a fully static system to anatomize and explain.

This book argues that there are parameters to disruptive innovation. These parameters are primarily historical and social. They are not primarily economic because this book focuses on technologies conforming to Christensen's core criteria, including cheap (1997, p. xv). This is not to argue that economic factors do not apply to technology adoption; Hargittai (2002, 2010), qualifying and contradicting the work of Prensky (2001), argues there is a digital divide but that it is constructed socio-economically. Instead, this book is more interested in how disruptive technologies influence learning and teaching practice in universities, and in how universities can engage constructively with disruptive technologies.

This book is also interested in contradictions within activity systems and what this signifies or illuminates. The book uses second generation activity theory (see next section), to use an Activity Theory term, as a tool to aid the examination of specific areas, especially the impact of disruptive technologies on the social nodes in an activity system, and perhaps most especially the impact of disruptive technologies on the division of labour in higher education and on the role of the university as gatekeeper to knowledge. Bakhurst (2009), in an otherwise critical account of Activity Theory, recognizes that Activity Theory can itself be used as a tool (p. 207).

Having examined Activity Theory, the next section discusses the development of Activity Theory into second generation Activity Theory and the theory of expansive learning.

SECOND GENERATION ACTIVITY THEORY: ENGESTRÖM AND EXPANSIVE LEARNING

This part of the chapter examines second generation Activity Theory and expansive learning. The discussion starts by looking at second generation Activity Theory before examining expansive learning separately. Thereafter, expansive learning is considered in relation to Disruptive Innovation, the specific role of tools in relation to Activity Theory is explored and Wikipedia is presented as a case study of Activity Theory and expansive learning.

Yrgo Engeström developed an expanded model of human activity to include and highlight the collaborative nature of practice, adding social elements to Vygotsky's original model of human activity, though Leontiev's image of the primeval hunt had already placed purposeful human activity within social contexts, especially the division of labour.

Engeström's second generation Activity Theory enables an exploration of how the use of disruptive technologies is ultimately collaborative. Second generation Activity Theory also enables analysis of how disruptive technologies impact on a community, its rules and its division of labour. Furthermore, Engeström focuses specifically on adult learning, as the original work on Activity Theory had concentrated on the issues of play and learning in children (Vygotsky 1978).

Engeström's book, *Learning by Expanding*, was first published in 1987 and revised in 2015. Engeström (2015) defines the two problems motivating his enquiry as 'the increasingly recognizable futility of learning in its standard reactive forms' and 'the elusive and uncontrollable nature of expansive processes where human beings transcend the contexts given to

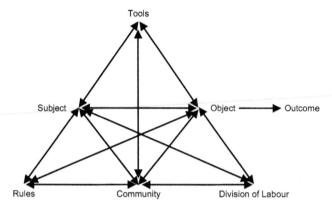

Fig. 3.2 The second generation activity system (After Engeström 1987, 2015, p. 63)

them' (p. 23). Engeström's representation of the activity system is shown below. (Fig. 3.2)

The model can be viewed as an ecosystem of purposeful human activity. The bottom row of the triangle (the layer added by Engeström) features the rules, the community and the division of labour as its nodes. The rules node represents the conventions and regulations shaping an activity, such as assessment within an education system. Community refers to those affected by the activity (primarily students and lecturers in the context of this book), also definable as 'the community of significant others' (Foot 2014, p. 331), 'multiple individuals who share the common general objectives' (Heo and Lee 2013, p. 135) or the 'sociocultural context in which the activity takes place' (Collis and Margaryan 2004, p. 41), and the division of labour node represents who does what in an activity, thereby illustrating both the distribution of tasks and the hierarchy of power, though not necessarily both at the same time; Kogut and Metiu (2001) show how the open software community has a division of labour but operates horizontally rather than vertically (p. 249). According to Jonassen and Rohrer-Murphy (1999), and despite the addition of social elements, the primary focus of the activity system remains the top triangle, where production is accomplished.

A more elaborate version of Engeström's second generation activity system triangle appears in Engeström (1993), is repeated by Roth and Lee (2007), features the 'higher order processes of production, exchange,

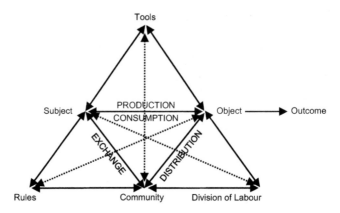

Fig. 3.3   Revised second generation activity system (After Engeström 1993, 2015, p. 63)

distribution and consumption' (Roth and Lee 2007, p. 197) and is shown below (Fig. 3.3):

The model incorporates an economic cycle of production, distribution and exchange, which is of less direct interest to this book, but which indicates how Disruptive Technology Enhanced Learning is implicated in a broad range of economic and social practices. The top of the triangle (subject, object and tool) is focused on production; exchange highlights the relationship between the subject and the community, while distribution relates primarily to the distribution of labour, as activities are sub-divided into individual actions undertaken by subjects. Moreover, Engeström (1993) argues, 'a human activity system always contains the subsystems of production, distribution, exchange, and consumption' (p. 67), indicating that these widest economic contexts are permanently implied in activity systems.

Engeström (2015) claims learning is unintentional and inevitable and identifies a mismatch between formal and real world learning, a position also taken from a Community of Practice perspective by Lave (1996). Formal education is a particular type of learning but does not have a monopoly on learning, a position later echoed by Wenger (1998) who argues learning is inevitable and ongoing, with teaching comprising one structuring resource for learning (p. 267). Vygotsky (1978) had constructed a similar argument when he wrote, 'even when, in the period of her first questions, a child assimilates the names of objects in her environment, she is learning ...

Learning and development are interrelated from the child's very first day of life' (p. 84). Learning is simply something humans do, and therefore it is appropriate to consider the kind of learning disruptive technologies facilitates, and to consider how disruptive technologies are a particular manifestation of human learning practice. Furthermore, the links between Engeström on the one hand, and Lave and Wenger on the other, illustrate a connection between Activity Theory and the Community of Practice theory, which will be explored in Chap. 4.

Westberry and Franken (2015) offer a distinctive definition of contradiction within an activity system as, 'a misalignment of interpretations of the object by different participants in the activity' (p. 300). In education, the idea of there being, in effect, more than one object is also explored by Mietinnen (1998); there is, for example, the object as constructed by the educator and the object as interpreted by the students (p. 424). Working back from the object, the educator may advocate the use of specific tools but students may use different tools, thereby generating a further contradiction within the tool node (potentially exacerbated by the role of marketing in the selection and usage of technologies), and a secondary contradiction between the tool and the division of labour, if students are by-passing sources identified by the lecturer and are, instead, opting for disruptive technologies to achieve the educational object as they perceive that object. For both Westberry and Franken (2015), and for Miettinen (1998), there is a hidden curriculum, but if we understand the hidden curriculum as a contradiction within the object node producing spin-out contradictions in other nodes and secondary contradictions between nodes, we can seek to resolve, or at least ameliorate, the contradiction by engaging constructively with disruptive technologies rather than forbidding or disapproving of their usage. We can, moreover, understand subjects' frustration if they are handed objects they have no part in constructing and are further handed a restricted set of tools to accomplish the object. Disruptive technologies comprise potent tools in activity systems, harboring the possibility for change.

A further feature of Engeström's (2015) argument is that activity is not only primary but also collaborative. Activities can be undertaken by individuals but the individual is always implicated in a range of historical and social discourses: 'Human labor, the mother form of all human activity, is co-operative from the very beginning' (pp. 53–54), a position echoing Leontiev (1981) and his image of the collaborative, primeval hunt (p. 187). Furthermore, and in this specific sense, Engeström's position overlaps with the Technology Acceptance Model. Bagozzi (2007) argues, 'we sometimes act seemingly as individuals spontaneously, deliberatively, or in response to social pressure. But perhaps more often than not we act interpersonally, or as agents of organizations, or jointly with others, or in a holistic sense as members of collectives. Decisions with regard to technology acceptance and actual usage are often done collaboratively or with an aim to how they fit in with, or affect, other people or group requisites' (p. 247). Activity can be individual but is at the same time necessarily social because, within the theoretical positions adopted in this book, individual consciousness is determined by its historical and social contexts. Jonassen and Rohrer-Murphy (1999) argue: 'Very little, if any, meaningful activity is accomplished individually. People may perform individually in contexts such as school, but their ability to perform is predicated on groups of people. The solo concert pianist, for instance, relies on teachers, the manufacturers of the piano, the designers and builders of the concert hall, and the accompanying conductor and orchestra ... Activities are complex and interactive, which necessitates collaborative effort' (p. 67). In this sense, this book is more aligned with Engeström's development of Activity Theory than with Leontiev's original formulation (though Kaptelinin (2005), in a close reading of Leontiev, accepts that all activities are considered by Leontiev to be social, even if they are not collaborative (p. 9)); where Leontiev talks about 'concrete individuals' (Kaptelinin 2005, p. 9), and Roth and Lee (2007) describe Activity Theory as a 'concrete psychology' (p. 192), this book think in terms of collage individuals, determined by a range of external historical and social factors. Bagozzi's (2007) use of the adverb 'seemingly' in his advocacy of the Technology Acceptance Model acknowledges that individual activity is more complex than it might at first appear.

Understandings of technology adoption that focus on the individual learner and teacher do not sit easily alongside an understanding of learning and teaching as social. It may be possible to design interventions (for example, training programmes for teachers) to change individual teacher beliefs over time, but that teacher will still be operating within social contexts. If we take the teacher, in second generation Activity Theory terms, as subject, an altered teacher belief as object and a designed intervention as the tool, we still need, within the second generation activity system, to factor in the social dimensions of rules, community and division of labour. The rules of the system within which the individual teacher operates may determine the technologies used and how they are used, the community of learners and teachers in which the teacher is implicated may have its own norms of technology usage, and the division of labour may also determine what technologies the teacher uses and how they use them. Therefore, the designed intervention by itself is not all-determining. Beliefs may shift but, this book argues, not mono-causally. Bagozzi (2007) accepts a weakness in the Technology Acceptance Model: 'technology acceptance research has not considered group, cultural or social aspects of decision making and usage very much' (p. 247). The adoption of technologies is, in line with Disruptive Innovation, Activity Theory and the Community of Practice theory, social, and determined historically. Meaningful change occurs through practice rather than technology design. Substantial, sustainable change is therefore a ground up process, as human subjects, through their practice with tools, pursue objects. More prosaically, people get jobs done using the tools at their disposal.

Expansive Learning

Expansive learning culminates in a full transformation of an activity system from the ground up, centring on the reformulation of the object. Engeström (2015) offers the following description of expansive learning:

> the process of expansive learning should be understood as construction and resolution of successively evolving contradictions in the activity system. The new concepts and practices generated by expansive learning activity are future-oriented visions loaded with initiative and commitment from below. They cannot be predefined and safely constrained by researchers or authorities. (Engeström, p. xx)

Engeström and Sannino (2011) outline how expansive learning unfolds and resolves: 'Inner contradictions need to be creatively and often painfully resolved by working out a qualitatively new "thirdness", something qualitatively different from a mere combination or compromise between two competing forces ... pushing the system into a new phase of development' (p. 371). In terms of the time expansive learning takes to accomplish, Engeström et al. (2007) argue, 'Big cycles of expansion typically last several years and generate qualitatively new models of work and organization' (p. 323), or, as Sannino et al. (2016) phrase it, expansive learning opens 'new, wider possibilities and responsibilities,' similar to Christensen's interpretation of the lengthy process of Disruptive Innovation (Christensen et al.

2015). Innovation, therefore, can be a painful process, as innovations expose, express and exacerbate contradictions within activity systems, the contradictions comprising an external manifestation of human subjects' thoughts and actions (Mietennen 1999, p. 174). With specific regard to technology enhanced learning in higher education, innovative practice may not align with institutional edict, forming individual tensions which may develop into contradictions over time. Innovation is fundamentally a ground up process, emerging out of practice rather than being decreed by authorities.

Contradictions create the conditions in which expansive learning can occur. Engeström and Sannino (2010) argue, 'Traditionally, we expect that learning is manifested as changes in the subject, i.e., in the behaviour and cognition of the learners. Expansive learning is manifested primarily as changes in the object of the collective activity' (p. 8). The object of higher education, definable as successful learning and teaching experiences and outcomes, appears fixed and therefore it may be more fruitful to consider how disruptive technology enhanced learning reformulates interactions in and between the social nodes in a second generation activity system, and how this impacts on subject and object. In this sense, this book posits a paradoxically sustaining innovation approach to Disruptive Technology Enhanced Learning, looking at how Disruptive Technology Enhanced Learning modifies the higher education activity system but does not seek its overthrow.

Engeström and Sannino (2010) offer a more formal, structured account of how expansive learning happens (p. 7). The first act is questioning. The second stage is analysis, trying to examine causes of the present situation. The third stage is to construct a model of a new idea. Stage four is analysis of the new model, and stage five, its implementation. Thereafter, the implementation of the new idea is reflected upon and evaluated (stage six), leading to its consolidation (stage seven). Questioning established practice is not always welcome in educational settings, but for Engeström and Sannino (2010) questioning is a necessary, formative stage for enabling the construction of new knowledge (p. 5). Moreover, their structural account of expansive learning provides a rudimentary framework that universities can use to work with disruptive technologies, observing and questioning technology practices and constructing and revising policies, rooted in students' and lecturers' actual practices with technologies.

To take an example, and applying the first stages of Engeström and Sannino's (2010) approach, many students and lecturers use Google.

Therefore, the question in the first instance might be why do students and lecturers use Google? The analysis, the second stage, could be the response to the question, that Google is a disruptive technology offering simplicity, ease of use and convenience at no direct financial cost to the user. The third stage, constructing a model of a new idea, could involve supporting students and lecturers in learning to use more sophisticated search tools and technologies, or, instead, the third stage might involve making proprietal technologies more like Google. Google itself has arguably taken up the second of these possibilities, through its implementation and development of Google Scholar, introduced in 2004. Stage four would involve the analysis of stage three, with stage five comprising its full, institutional roll-out. Stages six and seven would comprise the evaluation of Google as a tool for learning and teaching and its consolidation, perhaps by featuring in a university's technology enhanced learning strategy.

We could take the example further by looking at Google through a more sophisticated Activity Theory lens. The use of Google could be disapproved of by individual lecturers or the university as a whole because it challenges the standard research tools of the previous activity system, and hence contradictions arise between the new system and the remnants of the old. In addition, we can see Google as part of a suite of disruptive technologies representing wider changes in the learning and teaching practices of students and lecturers. Moreover, the movement of subjects between activity systems is conducive to innovation because the movement of subjects contains the potential for practices to cross borders and comprise innovations in their new context.

Change does not necessarily imply progress. This may be what Avis (2009) refers to when he argues that Activity Theory and expansive learning eschews the revolutionary implications of its own analysis, becoming instead a management technique (p. 161). Avis (2007) also argues that the emancipatory implications of Activity Theory are 'effectively bracketed' in Engeström's Activity Theory, that Engeström 'seeks to resolve peripheral rather than primary contradictions, thereby stopping short of radicalised practice,' and that, consequently, the changing of an existing activity system favours 'the functional rebel who performs an adaptive role' (Avis 2007, pp. 163, 164, 170); he goes so far as to describe Activity Theory as 'a form of consultancy aiming to improve work practices' (p. 169). Warmington (2008) argues similarly that Activity Theory 'underplays the wider social contradictions and antagonisms inherent in *commodification of labour power*' (p. 4, emphasis in original), and hence, 'its claims to produce transformative, expansive learning are heavily qualified' (p. 4). Engeström's and Sannino's (2010) less polemical argument implies that a technology can change practice partly but not fundamentally ('many transformations in activity systems are not predominantly expansive' p. 11). In Disruptive Technology Enhanced Learning, if the object of higher education remains the same, the resolution of peripheral contradictions is preferable to a reformulation of the object, especially if the latter course of action is not wanted by the community.

Engeström (1999a) recognizes the limitations of innovation in activity systems: 'Miniature cycles of innovative learning should be regarded as potentially expansive ... Small cycles may remain isolated events, and the overall cycle of organizational development may become stagnant, regressive or even fall apart' (p. 385), suggestive of Cortez's (2014) critique of novel financial securities instruments in relation to the 2008 financial crash as a disruptive innovation; innovation can be socially malign. Avis (2007) critiques Activity Theory and expansive learning when it understands without altering, but Benson and Whitworth (2007) see this as an asset, enabling full comprehension of a learning and teaching situation without insisting upon its radical overhaul. Avis's (2007) functional rebel can be anyone who tempers the use of technologies to suit a university's policies, but the tempering implies a lost opportunity to accelerate innovation. A malfunctioning or committed rebel can start a process of expansive learning through working with a disruptive technology. Warmington (2008) argues that Activity Theory's weakness is its 'downplaying of wider social antagonisms in favour of a truncated, technicist notion of contradictions' (p. 17), but there may be value in applying Activity Theory in individual instances without pursuing a full, expansive learning cycle.

Engeström (1999a) summarizes how expansive learning, 'begins with individual subjects questioning the accepted practice, and it gradually expands into a collective movement or institution' (p. 383); Roth and Lee (2007) argue, 'inner contradictions ... express themselves as trouble in ongoing activity' (p. 204). Therefore, instead of deviant behaviour being a sign of disorder to be quelled, Engeström's argument implies that apparently disruptive behaviour expresses the inadequacies of an existing system, requiring structural re-evaluation rather than castigation of an individual. Disruption, therefore, can be a call for wider change. For example, education systems have individuals who do not conform to the system. Engeström (2015) argues: 'The history of the school is also a history of inventing tricks for beating the system, and of protesting and breaking out.

... [T]oday's pupils are at an early age intensively drawn into the market as relatively independent consumers, even as producers ... (as computer hackers, as sport stars and performers, etc.). When the pupils' direct participation in the societal production is intensified, the "holding power" of the school is endangered' (pp. 82–83). Deviant behaviour within an activity system can signify the possibility of, or a need for, a new system for the production, distribution and exchange of knowledge, thereby linking Engeström's argument with Vygotsky's (1930) earlier stress on the value and transformative potential of education, and with Engeström's (1993) and Roth and Lee's (2007) more complex representation of the second generation activity system. Deviant behaviour comprises the tension which can, over time, become a contradiction in Engeström's terms, prompting a rethink of the object, and thus potentially producing expansive learning.

The contradictions between nodes in an activity system are central to expansive learning. For example, a lecturer (subject) works with students to achieve the object of high-quality learning. Technology (tools) can be used to enable the learning. However, if a new tool is available, over which the students, rather than the lecturer, have mastery, there are implications for the nodes on the bottom row; new practices within the activity system, such as a different division of labour, may be required in order for the object to be accomplished. Engeström (2001) argues, 'When an activity system adopts a new element from the outside ..., some old element (for example, the rules or the division of labor) collides with the new one. Such contradictions generate disturbances and conflicts, but also innovative attempts to change the activity' (p. 137). The analysis overlaps with Christensen's theory in the sense that a new technology can disrupt existing practices, thereby risking rejection, but also that the new technology can go on to change the practice itself. The object does not change in this instance and therefore the expansive cycle is incomplete, but there is a contradiction because it is not just the use of one technology creating a single tension but a range of technologies (for example, Google and Wikipedia) and practices (for example, Bring Your Own Device) that have changed aspects of the ways in which learning and teaching takes place.

A further, central characteristic of expansive learning is that it requires human agency. Therefore, while a contradiction is the starting point for expansive learning, the learning does not happen organically: 'Contradictions are the necessary but not sufficient engine of Expansive Learning in an activity system' (p. 7). Sannino et al. (2016) argue that a community 'needs to learn a dialectical methodology of transforming itself.' Contradictions evolve historically but they do not play out as a matter of historical necessity and, instead, require intervention to bring the expansive learning to fruition. At the level of the individual university, this could take the form of a technology enhanced learning strategy designed to recognize, engage with and promote the widespread use of disruptive technologies (UK university technology enhanced learning strategies are surveyed in Chap. 5), though Engeström et al. (2013) argue that interventionists do not mechanically determine the outcome.

Despite their uncertainty, contradictions are ultimately a sign of a healthy and living activity system; Whitworth (2005) argues, 'Conflict within organisations is inevitable, but without conflict there would be no creativity, and hence no innovation' (p. 690). Therefore, a characteristic feature of expansive learning and Activity Theory is that, 'it acknowledges contradictions, conflict, and breakdowns in coordination as inevitable in the functioning of any system' (Foot 2014, p. 337). Progress depends upon conflict and Disruptive Technology Enhanced Learning is thus a necessary and progressive feature of learning and teaching in higher education.

Engeström et al. (2013) use figurative language to describe change in an activity system: 'a path emerging within a texture of various bypaths, or as a melody taking shape among background sounds and complementary, perhaps also competing tunes' (p. 92), defining expansive learning as 'punctuated by deviations' (p. 81). Expansive learning requires human agency but it is also an unpredictable process, a position which aligns with Disruptive Innovation, which emerges from practice rather than policy. There are parameters to disruptive innovation, determined by a range of factors, most notably existing practice determined, in turn, by historical practice. Disruption is not the unfettered expression of creativity. Similarly, expansive learning is not unbounded but is managed through direct human agency in combination with broader historical factors.

Expansive Learning and Disruptive Innovation

Expansive learning is disruptive. The distinctive feature of expansive learning is that it starts with an act of dissent, or with the critical interrogation of an accepted and established practice (Engeström 1999a, p. 383). Disruptive technologies can be culturally anomalous at first, such as the Honda Super Cub in an American motorcycle culture dominated by Harley Davidson machines (Christensen 1997), or the technically inferior reception of a Sony transistor radio (Bower and Christensen 1995; Christensen and Raynor

2003; Christensen et al. 2008); disruptive technologies assert their own applicability by changing, however locally, a practice and thus a wider activity system or culture. In both of the examples given, the practice of users created a purpose and disrupted an established market.

Engeström and Sannino (2011) argue, 'contradictions cannot be observed directly; they can only be identified through their manifestations' (p. 369). If we understand these manifestations as changes in practice, we can read a contradiction in Engeström's sense as an innovation in Christensen's sense. The innovation appears irregular at first but becomes, over time, mainstream as its suitability and usefulness to its context is recognized. Engeström's argument also aligns with Christensen's (1997) analysis of disruptive technologies, which disrupt an existing commercial or educational system and seem anomalous at first, but become accepted and indeed displace an incumbent product or service, becoming, in time, sustaining technologies, familiar to users and improving incrementally. Engeström (2015) uses the metaphor of a springboard to describe the movement forward (p. 226) but acknowledges that the resultant change may not resemble the initial springboard. The moment of change, the catalyst, is fundamentally important.

Linking Activity Theory and expansive learning to disruptive technologies and disruptive innovation, disruptive technologies often begin by appealing to a small number of users, those who question, through their technology usage, existing practices, and the use of the disruptive technology can thus accelerate and, in so doing, change a broader practice, thus implying the potential for an expansive learning cycle. The object of the Honda Super Cub (see Chap. 2) changed as subjects' views of the tool changed, from utilitarian to recreational, creating a new object and thus completing an expansive cycle in the field of goods and services. Disruptive Technology Enhanced Learning has the potential to change higher education, if not currently at the level of object in an activity system, then certainly at the level of the rules, community and division of labour nodes in a second generation activity system, by introducing practices that differ from established practices of research and assessment.

This reading of expansive learning links with the formative work on Activity Theory, because if consciousness is socially constructed, as Vygotsky (1930) and Leontiev (1977) argue, individual psychological problems are manifestations of underlying conflicts in social relations. Extending the argument, the usage of technologies is social rather than individual and the disruptive use of a technology is the result of a social pressure which may express itself through an individual's practice, but without the disruption being the product of a sole, individual consciousness.

TOOLS IN ACTIVITY THEORY

Engeström (2015) argues, 'A tool always implies more possible uses than the original operations that have given birth to it' and 'the same artefact may have different meanings depending on the context' (pp. 115 and 185). These qualifications by Engeström are relevant because they indicate that engagement with disruptive technologies is a dynamic process with the potential to change individuals. The technologies deployed to undertake jobs in support of learning and teaching in higher education have an impact on subjects, objects and social relations. Lawrence (2015) argues that students' research practices have changed in the digital age, hence the widespread use of Google and Wikipedia by both students and lecturers (see also, Flavin 2012, 2016). Disruptive technologies have changed subjects' practices in higher education because the technologies have acquired a purpose in higher education, even though they may not necessarily have been designed for higher education.

A key aspect of Vygotsky's and Engeström's understanding of the interaction between subjects and tools is that tools are not the passive recipients of human action. Instead, tools are 'integral and inseparable components of human functioning' (Engeström 1999b, p. 29). Technologies are essentially inert until they are drawn into human actions (Engeström and Glăveanu (2012) argue, 'No tool achieves anything by itself.' (p. 517)) but, once drawn into actions, tools shape as well as are shaped (Engeström 2007), not least because the tools carry with them traces of previous human action and innovation, in the sense that they will have been designed to undertake particular jobs in particular contexts. This is presumably what Daniels (2014) means when he writes, 'A theory of mediation through artefacts infers that in the course of human activity meaning is sedimented, accumulated or deposited in things' (p. 22); activity does not occur in an unfettered space but in a historically saturated space.

The uses to which technology tools are put is a matter of practice, not design: 'the material form and shape of the artifact have only limited power to determine its epistemic use' (Engeström 2007, pp. 34–35). This leads Engeström to conclude, 'In Expansive Learning ... reconfiguration of given technologies by their users is essential' (p. 35). Subjects explore and define the meanings of technologies through their uses of them and meaning is not constrained by design, an argument also presented by Christensen and Raynor (2003) though, according to Activity Theory, use and therefore meaning are shaped by historical development. Moreover, and in common with Wenger (1998, pp. 227, 233) from a Community of Practice perspective, Engeström argues that learning requires imagination, improvisation and innovation.

An evaluation of the effectiveness of a technology tool involves considering how it impacts on other nodes in an activity system. Social media technologies, for example, have the potential to transform learning and teaching through enhanced student engagement and personal interaction (Hoffman 2009), but this may not be what users want (which is what this book argues), as users wish to keep their learning and teaching lives separate from their recreational lives, a position also noted in the sample of 213 students in Madge et al. (2009), and positively encouraged in relation to medical practitioners in the USA (Mostaghimi and Crotty 2011), but contradicted by some of the studies summarized in Manca and Ranieri (2013). That said, subsequent original research by Manca and Ranieri (2016) shows over 6000 academic staff in Italy adopting conservative uses of social media. Users, by and large, do not see Facebook and other social media technologies as a means of achieving primarily educational objects, but social objects. Social media technologies may be supporting learning and teaching in higher education, but they are not transforming it.

WIKIPEDIA AND ACTIVITY THEORY

Some of my own research has aligned Activity Theory and expansive learning with disruptive technologies and Disruptive Innovation. For example, questionnaires I issued showed Wikipedia being used as a tool in an Activity Theory sense, as students and lecturers were using it to get jobs done (Flavin 2012, p. 106). The simplicity and convenience of Wikipedia plays a part in its usage, thus also suggesting the validity of Christensen's core criteria for disruptive technologies (Christensen 1997, p. xv). Furthermore, the use of Wikipedia as a tool creates tension between the tools node of the second generation activity system and the division of labour node because reading lists and academic libraries can be bypassed, though, in practice, the participants seemed capable of managing the tension (Flavin 2012, p. 10; 2016, p. 11).

The use of Wikipedia as a disruptive technology in higher education has implications for the rules and community of the university if material accessed through Wikipedia informs work submitted for assessment (Flavin 2016, p. 8); the use of a publication without editorial oversight is not approved of in conventional academic practice. Engeström (2009) also comments on the relevance of Wikipedia for an Activity Theory and expansive learning analysis: 'Wikipedia is a good example in that every alteration of an entry is automatically stored and retrievable for anyone as a cumulative record of previous versions and alterations' (p. 4), though his argument draws attention to the way knowledge is deposited and sedimented in Wikipedia, with any tensions being audited.

Wikipedia is a palimpsest, a text that carries traces of previous text within it. Its primary contradiction is thus apparent from a cursory examination of Wikipedia's mode of production. Wikipedia's secondary contradiction focuses on the tools node and the division of labour node, as the use of the tool disrupts the traditional division of academic labour. Wikipedia's tertiary contradiction rests in its potential to disrupt established forms of academic production, distribution and consumption; Wikipedia is collaboratively authored, distributed without mediation through an academic library and is used to get jobs done in preference to previously established academic sources, thus creating tension between an emerging activity system and an existing activity system. Moreover, there is a potential quaternary contradiction if Wikipedia is representative of the use of disruptive technologies in higher education and can be considered in relation to other disruptive technologies. Overall, Wikipedia's status as a palimpsest highlights potential contradiction; the different traces, residues and contributions entail tensions and different perspectives. Wikipedia is always a contested space for the production of knowledge. Moreover, Wikipedia's convenience, ease of use (and the fact that it is free to use) highlights its status as a disruptive technology. Wikipedia as a disruptive technology can be analysed from an Activity Theory perspective to understand how its usage impacts on higher education practice. However, from an expansive learning perspective, Wikipedia is not changing the object of higher education; it disrupts relationships between specific nodes but the object remains the same, primarily because the existing object has clear relevance and use value.

The figure below demonstrates Wikipedia as a disruptive technology within the framework of Engeström's second generation Activity Theory (Fig. 3.4).

The figure focuses on the tertiary contradiction of Wikipedia. The upper triangle of subject, tool and object indicates Wikipedia is used in arterial

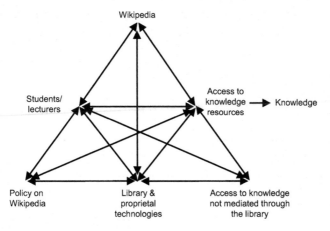

Fig. 3.4 Wikipedia as a disruptive technology

ways by students and lecturers wanting to get jobs done, but the nodes on the bottom row of the triangle highlight the issues generated by the use of Wikipedia as well as highlighting the complexity of its usage because it can prompt a rethink of the university. Universities continue to control learning and teaching through assessment and awards but are less directive of the day-to-day learning and teaching taking place in practice. A contradiction between the object of institutional higher education and the tools used to that end can change the relationship between subject and object, as the subject is not dependent on the primary feature of the community (the university itself) to achieve educational objects. Eijkman (2010) argues, 'Wikipedia ... is inimical to conventional power-knowledge arrangements in which academics are traditionally positioned as the key gatekeepers to knowledge' (p. 173), recognizing that Wikipedia challenges the traditional academic division of labour.

It is also possible to analyse Wikipedia through the more complex representation of the second generation activity system, including production, distribution and exchange. The relationship between subject, tool and object centres on the production and consumption of knowledge, yet the division of labour in Wikipedia also relates to production and consumption as well as distribution, because knowledge is produced and consumed in Wikipedia in the context of a relationship that can change the established division of labour in higher education. That said, the relationship between subject and community in Wikipedia usage does centre on exchange. The limited applicability of the more sophisticated representation of the second generation activity system to Wikipedia might highlight the limitations of the model, though it might also underline the status of Wikipedia as a disruptive technology, exemplifying a transformation of learning and teaching practice in higher education, through technology.

To take another example, the object for Twitter is normally identified through practice and hence its object is not the same for all users. Twitter thus has the potential for expansive learning because the identification of the object, a primary act (Engeström 2015, p. 254), will influence, though not absolutely determine, the other nodes in activity system. Twitter was perceived to be more convenient than an institutional VLE for biological sciences students surveyed by Jacquemin et al. (2014, p. 25), thus helping to identify Twitter as a potentially disruptive technology that can be appropriated for educational use. Junco et al. (2013) present an instance of Twitter being successfully integrated into a university course but in the context of 'a theoretically driven pedagogical model' (p. 273). A more interesting approach might be to allow practice from the ground up to determine purpose. Twitter has disruptive technology potential and expansive learning potential, but it does not necessarily follow that it is a disruptive technology or that it will result in expansive learning.

To consider Activity Theory in relation to other technologies, two respondents to a questionnaire I issued (Flavin 2012) were interviewed and introduced to a new (to them) technology and were interviewed again 10 months later. One had created a purpose for the technology to which she had been introduced (Delicious, free bookmarking software) and the other had not found a purpose for the technology to which she had been introduced (Wallwisher, free online notice board). The creation of a purpose is important from the point of view of Disruptive Innovation but it is central in Activity Theory because it comprises the identification of an object and the role of the tool in attaining the object. Without a clear object, the other nodes cannot take shape (Engeström 2015, p. 201), the object identifying and defining the activity as a whole (Engeström 2015, pp. 201, 254). Vygotsky's original triad of subject, tool and object is thus still valid and primary, as without an object the subject cannot construct a clear purpose for a tool, unless imaginative play without an a priori object leads to the construction of an object through practice, thus linking Disruptive Innovation and Activity Theory. An object can be produced by a subject's practice, rather than its being decreed, but an object needs to exist in order for the other nodes in an activity system to have clear definition and substance.

KEY POINTS FROM EXPANSIVE LEARNING

Expansive learning argues that contradictions within activity systems are necessary if not sufficient precursors to and catalysts of change. The analysis of contradictions is linked with disruptive technologies, identifying technology tools that are not specifically designed for educational purposes but which are used to support learning and teaching, being repurposed by their users. Furthermore, second generation Activity Theory based on the theory of expansive learning argues for the multi-voicedness of activity systems implying that collaboration is key to the successful execution of any activity, including learning and teaching in higher education, and using technologies.

Daniels (2008), following Engeström (1999b, 2001), outlines Activity Theory with the help of five principles. The first is the activity system seen in network relations to other activity systems. The second is multi-voicedness; activity systems embody different perspectives and interests. The third principle is historicity; activity systems evolve and transform over time. The fourth principle is that contradictions are central as sources of change and development. The final principle is the possibility of expansive transformation in activity systems. This book recognizes contradictions and thus development within activity systems, partly through recognizing the centrality of practice in the creation of purposes for the use of technologies. The book also focuses on recognizing and exploring contradictions; the book also recognizes possibilities for transformation through the use of technology tools. The activity system of students differs frequently from the activity system of the university, as students use simple and convenient tools to support their learning and assessment (Lawrence 2015; Selwyn and Gorard 2016), assessment comprising an aspect of the rules node of the activity system. Students' perspectives and interests can differ from the university's perspective and interests, not least because students seek efficient, simple and convenient means of getting jobs done, preferably without financial cost. There is, moreover, a symbiosis between the popular disruptive technologies Google and Wikipedia, as, 'One feature of the Google results that students have come to rely upon is the appearance of a Wikipedia result at the top of the first page' (Lawrence 2015, p. 91). The first paragraph of a Wikipedia entry is commonly written in lay terms, thus providing a simple

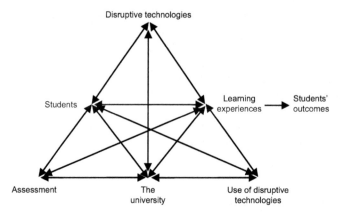

Fig. 3.5   Disruptive technologies in the university activity system

and convenient technology solution, a tool to get a job done or at least started.

Google and Wikipedia can be seen as complementary activity systems as well as disruptive technologies or, internally, as complementary tools within the same activity system under the heading of disruptive technologies. Taking a university as an activity system, with the object of successful learning experiences and outcomes, the perspectives of the university and its students do not necessarily conflate, an argument also made by Westberry and Franken (2015). The contradictions implicit in the use of Google and Wikipedia signify a transformation in how research is done in the twenty-first century. Treating the university as a community and treating technologies such as Google and Wikipedia as disruptive technologies, the following second generation activity system is possible (Fig. 3.5):

This figure indicates how a tension between disruptive technologies and the division of labour on one hand, and the university community on the other, can serve successful experiences and outcomes from students' point of view, or compromise experiences and outcomes from the university's perspective. The object does not change, but practice and relationships within the activity system do change.

To apply a more sophisticated second generation Activity Theory analysis, there are tensions between disruptive technologies and the established division of labour relating to production, consumption and distribution. By distributing labour differently, knowledge is produced and consumed in different ways without necessary mediation through a lecturer or reading list. By recognizing different patterns of production, consumption and distribution, the community can reconceptualize the use of technology to support learning and teaching.

Disruptive technologies can also comprise an additional voice in the sense of an additional source of information (or, in Activity Theory terms, a tool), not owned or controlled by the university but adding to existing voices. For example, reading lists for modules and programmes can be supplemented or even supplanted by resources located via disruptive technologies. Universities are in a position to engage constructively with disruptive technologies and an expansive learning approach enables consideration of how disruptive technologies can create new practices in learning and teaching. Engeström (2015) argues, 'A genuine expansive cycle inevitably produces not only civilization but also an ingredient of wilderness. To gain a theoretical grasp of this wilderness, to find and understand something unexpected as a piece of the history of the future is the reward' (p. 252). Engeström and Sannino (2010) state that, in expansive learning, 'learners learn something that is not yet there' (p. 2). Expansive learning is an uncertain process because it exposes contradictions, but in so doing it can create systems of learning and teaching appropriate for emerging social contexts.

CONCLUSION

This chapter has surveyed different aspects and interpretations of Activity Theory in relation to core ideas in the book. There are numerous interpretations of Activity Theory, a fact which is identified as a strength by Kaptelinin (2005): 'the differences between these complementary activity-theoretical perspectives should be judged not as a disadvantage of activity theory but as an indicator of diversity, interdisciplinarity, multivoicedness, and developmental potential of the approach' (p. 12). Engeström (1993) also recognizes that Activity theory is not a 'fixed and finished' body of work (p. 64).

This chapter has related Activity Theory and expansive learning to disruptive technologies and Disruptive Innovation, a synthesis which has also been attempted by Yamagata-Lynch et al. (2015), who argue, 'activity systems analysis can highlight the complex and chaotic interactions involved in the transformation of disruptive to sustaining technology' (p. 17). Activity Theory is ultimately an optimistic framework because it identifies where tensions and potential contradictions lie, and thus makes their resolution possible, enabling change as well as explanation. As Roth (2004) argues, Activity Theory 'embodies much needed hope. Rather than accepting circumstances as they are ... it encourages us to view each action also as transformational – changing the life conditions and ourselves' (p. 7). This chapter has interwoven aspects of Activity Theory with Disruptive Innovation, and has anticipated connections between Activity Theory and the subject of the next chapter, the Community of Practice theory. Westberry and Franklin (2015), from an Activity Theory perspective, argue, 'learning is viewed as participation with others within a particular sociocultural context rather than learning as the acquisition of individual cognitive processes' (p. 302), a position which almost conflates with the definition of learning in a community of practice, as we shall see.

REFERENCES

Avis, J. (2007). Engeström's version of activity theory: A conservative praxis? *Journal of Education and Work, 20*(3), 161–177.

Avis, J. (2009). Transformation or transformism: Engeström's version of activity theory? *Educational Review, 61*(2), 151–165.

Bagozzi, R. P. (2007). The legacy of the technology acceptance model and a proposal for a paradigm shift. *Journal of the Association for Information Systems, 8*(4), 244–254.

Bakhurst, D. (2009). Reflections on activity theory. *Educational Review, 61*(2), 197–210.

Bennett, L. (2010). *Activity theory: What does it offer elearning research?* University of Huddersfield repository. Retrieved from http://eprints.hud.ac.uk/10631/

Benson, A., & Whitworth, A. (2007). Technology at the planning table: Activity theory, negotiation and course management systems. *Journal of Organisational Transformation and Social Change, 4*(1), 75–92.

Bower, J. L., & Christensen, C. M. (1995). Disruptive technologies: Catching the wave. *Harvard Business Review, 1*(13), 43–53.

Christensen, C. M. (1997). *The innovator's dilemma: When new technologies cause great firms to fail.* Boston: Harvard Business School Press.

Christensen, C. M., & Raynor, M. E. (2003). *The innovator's solution: Creating and sustaining successful growth.* Boston: Harvard Business School Press.

Christensen, C. M., Horn, M. B., & Johnson, C. W. (2008). *Disrupting class: How disruptive innovation will change the way the world learns.* New York: McGraw-Hill.

Christensen, C. M., Raynor, M. E., & McDonald, R. (2015). What is disruptive innovation? *Harvard Business Review, 93*(12), 44–53.

Collis, B., & Margaryan, A. (2004). Applying activity theory to computer-supported collaborative learning and work-based activities in corporate settings. *Educational Technology Research and Development, 52*(4), 38–52.

Cortez, N. (2014). Regulating disruptive innovation. *Berkeley Technology Law Journal, 29*(1), 175–228.

Czerniewicz, L., Glover, M., Deacon, A., & Walji, S. (2016). MOOCs, openness and changing educator practices: An Activity Theory case study. In S. Cranmer, N. B. Dohn, M. de Laat, T. Ryberg & J. A. Sime (Eds.), *Proceedings of the 10th international conference on networked learning 2016* (pp. 287–294).

Daniels, H. (2008). *Vygotsky and research.* Abingdon: Routledge.

Daniels, H. (2014). Vygotsky and dialogic pedagogy. *Cultural-Historical Psychology, 10*(3), 19–29.

Eijkman, H. (2010). Academics and Wikipedia: Reframing Web2.0+ as a disruptor of traditional academic power-knowledge arrangements. *Campus-Wide Information Systems, 27*(3), 173–185.

Engeström, Y. (1987). *Learning by expanding: An activity-theoretical approach to developmental research.* Helsinki: Orienta-Konsultit Oy. Retrieved from http://lchc.ucsd.edu/MCA/Paper/Engestrom/expanding/toc.htm

Engeström, Y. (1993). Developmental studies of work as a testbench of activity theory: The case of primary care medical practice. In S. Chaiklin & J. Lave (Eds.), *Understanding practice: Perspectives on activity and context* (pp. 64–103). Cambridge: Cambridge University Press.

Engeström, Y. (1999a). Innovative learning in work teams: Analyzing cycles of knowledge creation in practice. In Y. Engeström, R. Miettinen, & R. L. Punamaki (Eds.), *Perspectives on activity theory* (pp. 377–406). Cambridge: Cambridge University Press.

Engeström, Y. (1999b). Activity theory and individual and social transformation. In Y. Engeström, R. Miettinen, & R. L. Punamaki (Eds.), *Perspectives on activity theory* (pp. 19–38). Cambridge: Cambridge University Press.

Engeström, Y. (2001). Expansive learning at work: Toward an activity theoretical reconceptualization. *Journal of Education and Work, 14*(1), 133–156.

Engeström, Y. (2007). Enriching the theory of expansive learning: Lessons from journeys toward coconfiguration. *Mind, Culture and Activity, 14*(1–2), 23–39.

Engeström, Y. (2009). Wildfire activities: New patterns of mobility and learning. *International Journal of Mobile and Blended Learning, 1*(2), 1–18.

Engeström, Y. (2015). *Learning by expanding: An activity-theoretical approach to developmental research* (2nd ed.). New York: Cambridge University Press.

Engeström, Y., & Glăveanu, V. (2012). On third generation activity theory: Interview with Yrgo Engeström. *Europe's Journal of Psychology, 8*(4), 515–518.

Engeström, Y., & Miettenen, R. (1999). Introduction. In Y. Engeström, R. Miettenen, & R.-L. Punamäki (Eds.), *Perspectives on activity theory* (pp. 1–18). Cambridge: Cambridge University Press.

Engeström, Y., & Sannino, A. (2010). Studies of expansive learning: Foundation, findings and future challenges. *Educational Research Review, 5,* 1–24.

Engeström, Y., & Sannino, A. (2011). Discursive manifestations of contradictions in organizational change efforts. *Journal of Organizational Change Management, 24*(3), 368–387.

Engeström, Y., Kersuo, H., & Kajamaa, A. (2007). Beyond discontinuity: Expansive organizational learning remembered. *Management Learning, 38*(3), 319–336.

Engeström, Y., Rantavuori, J., & Kerosuo, H. (2013). Expansive learning in a library: Actions, cycles and deviations from instructional intentions. *Vocations and Learning, 6,* 81–106.

Flavin, M. (2012). Disruptive technologies in higher education. *Research in Learning Technology, 20,* 102–111.

Flavin, M. (2016). Disruptive conduct: The impact of disruptive technologies on social relations in higher education. *Innovations in Education and Teaching International, 15*(1), 3–15.

Foot, K. A. (2014). Cultural-historical activity theory: Exploring a theory to inform practice and research. *Journal of Human Behavior in the Social Environment, 24*(3), 329–347.

Gay, G., Rieger, R., & Bennington, T. (2001). Using mobile computing to enhance field study. In T. Koschmann, R. Hall, & N. Miyake (Eds.), *CSCL2: Carrying forward the conversation.* Mahwah: Lawrence Erlbaum.

Hargittai, E. (2002). Second level digital divide. *First Monday, 7*(4). Retrieved from http://firstmonday.org/htbin/cgiwrap/bin/ojs/index.php/fm/article/view/942/864

Hargittai, E. (2010). Digital na(t)ives? Variation in internet skills and uses among members of the "net generation". *Sociological Inquiry, 80*(1), 92–114.

Heo, G. M., & Lee, R. (2013). Blogs and social network sites as activity systems: Exploring adult informal learning process through activity theory framework. *Educational Technology and Society, 16*(4), 133–145.

Hoffman, E. S. (2009). Evaluating social networking tools for distance learning. *Proceedings of the 2009 Technology, Colleges and Community (TCC) Conference.* Retrieved from http://etec.hawaii.edu/proceedings/2009/hoffman.pdf

Hu, P., Clark, T., & Ma, W. (2003). Examining technology acceptance by school teachers: A longitudinal study. *Information Management, 41*(2), 227–241.

Huizinga, J. (1971, original work published 1938). *Homo Ludens.* Boston: Beacon Press.

Hung, D. W. L., & Chen, D.-T. (2001). Situated cognition, Vygotskian thought and learning from the communities of practice perspective: Implications for the design of web-based e-learning. *Educational Media International, 38*(1), 3–12.

Jacquemin, S. L., Smelser, L. K., & Bernot, M. J. (2014). Twitter in the higher education classroom: A student and faculty assessment of use and perception. *Journal of College Science Teaching, 43*(6), 22–27.

Jonassen, D. H., & Rohrer-Murphy, L. (1999). Activity theory as a framework for designing constructivist learning environments. *Educational Technology Research and Development, 47*(1), 61–79.

Junco, R., Elavsky, C. M., & Heiberger, G. (2013). Putting Twitter to the test: Assessing outcomes for student collaboration, engagement and success. *British Journal of Educational Technology, 44*(2), 273–287.

Kaptelinin, V. (2005). The object of activity: Making sense of the sense-maker. *Mind, Culture and Activity, 12*(1), 4–18.

Kogut, B., & Metiu, A. (2001). Open-source software development and distributed innovation. *Oxford Review of Economic Policy, 17*(2), 248–269.

Krejsler, J. (2004). Becoming individual in education and cyberspace. *Teachers and Teaching: Theory and Practice, 10*(5), 489–503.

Lave, J. (1996). Teaching, as learning, in practice. *Mind, Culture and Activity, 3*(3), 149–164.

Lawrence, K. (2015). Today's college students: Skimmers, scanners and efficiency-seekers. *Information Services and Use, 35*, 89–93.

Leontiev, A. N. (1977). Activity and consciousness. In *Philosophy of the USSR, problems of dialectical materialism* (trans. Daglish, R.). Moscow: Progress. Retrieved from https://www.marxists.org/archive/leontev/works/1977/leon1977.htm

Leontiev, A. N. (1978). *Activity, consciousness and personality* (trans. Hall, M.J.). Englewood Cliffs: Prentice Hall.

Leontiev, A. N. (1981). *Problems of the development of the mind.* Moscow: Progress.

Madge, C., Meek, J., Wellens, J., & Hooley, T. (2009). Facebook, social integration and informal learning at university: It is more for socialising and talking to friends about work than for actually doing work. *Learning, Media and Technology, 34*(2), 141–155.

Manca, S., & Ranieri, M. (2013). Is it a tool suitable for learning? A critical review of the literature on Facebook as a technology-enhanced learning environment. *Journal of Computer Assisted Learning, 29*(6), 487–504.

Manca, S., & Ranieri, M. (2016). Facebook and the others. Potentials and obstacles of social media for teaching in higher education. *Computers and Education, 95*, 216–230.

Markides, C. (2006). Disruptive innovation; in need of better theory. *The Journal of Product Innovation Management, 23*, 19–25.

Miettinen, R. (1998). Object construction and networks in research work: The case of research on cellulose-degrading enzymes. *Social Studies of Science, 28*(3), 423–463.

Miettinen, R. (1999). The riddle of things: Activity theory and actor-network theory as approaches to studying innovations. *Mind, Culture, and Activity, 6*(3), 170–195.

Mostaghimi, A., & Crotty, B. H. (2011). Professionalism in the digital age. *Annals of Internal Medicine, 154*(8), 560–562.

Prensky, M. (2001). Digital natives, digital immigrants. *On the Horizon, 9*(5). Retrieved from http://www.marcprensky.com/writing/prensky%20-%20digi tal%20natives,%20digital%20immigrants%20-%20part1.pdf

Roth, W. M. (2004). Activity theory and education: An introduction. *Mind, Culture, and Activity, 11*(1), 1–8.

Roth, W. M. (2007). Emotion at work: A contribution to third-generation cultural historical activity theory. *Mind, Culture, and Activity, 14*, 40–63.

Roth, W. M., & Lee, Y. J. (2007). "Vygotsky's neglected legacy": Cultural-historical activity theory. *Review of Educational Research, 77*(2), 186–232.

Rückriem, G. (2010). Digital technology, mediation, and activity theory. *Cultural-Historical Psychology, 4*, 30–38.

Sannino, A., Engeström, Y., & Lahikainen, J. (2016). The dialectics of authoring expansive learning: Tracing the long tail of a change laboratory. *Journal of Workplace Learning, 28*(4), 245–262.

Selwyn, N., & Gorard, S. (2016). Students' use of Wikipedia as an academic resource – Patterns of use and patterns of usefulness. *Internet and Higher Education, 28*, 28–34.

Smagorinsky, P. H. (2009). The culture of Vygotsky. *Reading Research Quarterly, 44*(1), 85–95.

Spinuzzi, C. (2014). How nonemployer firms stage-manage Ad-Hoc collaboration: An activity theory analysis. *Technical Communication Quarterly, 23*(2), 88–114.

Vygotsky, L. (1930). The socialist alteration of man. In R. Van Der Veet & J. Valsiner (Eds.), *The Vygotsky reader* (pp. 175–184). Oxford: Blackwell.

Vygotsky, L. S. (1978). In M. Cole, V. John-Steiner, S. Scribner, & E. Souberman (Eds.), *Mind in society: The development of higher psychological processes*. London: Harvard University Press.

Warmington, P. (2008). From "activity" to "labour": Commodification, labour-power and contradiction in Engeström's activity theory. *Outlines: Critical Practice Studies, 10*(2), 4–19.

Wenger, E. (1998). *Communities of practice: Learning, meaning, and identity*. Cambridge: Cambridge University Press.

Westberry, N., & Franken, M. (2015). Pedagogical distance: Explaining misalignment in student-driven online learning activities using Activity Theory. *Teaching in Higher Education, 20*(3), 300–312.

Whitworth, A. (2005). Colloquium. *British Journal of Educational Technology, 36* (4), 685–691.

Yamagata-Lynch, L. C., Cowan, J., & Luetkehans, L. M. (2015). Transforming disruptive technology into sustainable technology: Understanding the front-end design of an online program at a brick-and-mortar university. *Internet and Higher Education, 26*, 1–18.

CHAPTER 4

Whatever Happened to the Digital Natives? Disruptive Innovation in the Higher Education Community of Practice

INTRODUCTION

Marc Prensky's hypothesis of digital natives and digital immigrants (2001) was, at the time, highly influential. In essence, it argued for a generationally constituted digital divide. Intuitively, Prensky's hypothesis feels accurate, as though it reflects common sense and day-to-day reality; parents are often taken aback by the technological adeptness of their children. However, Prensky's (2001) hypothesis was not based on primary research. Furthermore, once research in the area of digital natives and digital immigrants was undertaken it tended, surprisingly, to refute Prensky, commonly finding no significant generational difference in the use of digital technologies (Bennett et al. 2008; Jones and Healing 2010; Corrin et al. 2010; Margaryan et al. 2011; Somyürek and Coşkun 2013); Selwyn (2009) argues, 'young people's engagements with digital technologies are ... often unspectacular – in stark contrast to popular portrayals of the digital native' (p. 364), while Henderson et al. (2015) recognize that 'university students comprise a wide spectrum of digital competence' (p. 308). That said, research by Hargittai (2002, 2010) has found a digital divide, but constructed socio-economically rather than generationally, with users from privileged backgrounds tending to use the internet more widely and effectively than their less privileged peers. Instead of conceptualizing technology usage in dichotomous, gen erational terms, therefore, this chapter conceptualizes technology usage in terms of community membership and in

© The Author(s) 2017
M. Flavin, *Disruptive Technology Enhanced Learning*,
DOI 10.1057/978-1-137-57284-4_4

87

terms of how the use of disruptive technologies aids or impedes progress within and core membership of a higher education community. The chapter uses the Community of Practice theory as a means of understanding how disruptive technologies impact on university communities, recognizing that a range of stakeholders contribute to learning and teaching. More specifically, the chapter uses Lave and Wenger's (1991) and Wenger's (1998) work on legitimate peripheral participation and on the Community of Practice to understand how disruptive technologies can enable or impede progress within a community, especially for students. The chapter is also interested in how technologies are used to construct and negotiate identities in communities of practice, and in the significance of legitimate peripheral participation in learning communities, especially as it relates to innovation. In addition, the chapter engages with critique of the Community of Practice in order to offer a nuanced reading of the theory in relation to Disruptive Technology Enhanced Learning in higher education, as well as considering the tension between design for learning on one hand, and practice on the other, in communities of practice.

The chapter also links the Community of Practice theory with Activity Theory by using the Community of Practice as a means of illuminating the community node of an activity system and by exploring tensions within communities of practice. While Activity Theory is represented as a triangle, the standard community of practice model may be better thought of as a circle, with individual human subjects moving from the periphery to the community's centre, the locus of expertise. The chapter is also interested in the community node of an activity system as the locus of innovation. The chapter concludes by considering Wikipedia as a community of practice and by anticipating the synthesis of Disruptive Innovation, Activity Theory and the Community of Practice in the book's conclusion, in relation to Disruptive Technology Enhanced Learning.

THE COMMUNITY OF PRACTICE

The term Community of Practice derives from work by Lave and Wenger (1991), who argue that learners start on the periphery of communities and travel towards the centre. Good progress relies on a supportive structure within the community.

The original research of Lave and Wenger (1991) had looked at learning in a variety of contexts, from West African tailors to indigenous American midwives to trainee butchers to Alcoholics Anonymous, and had concluded that learning traces a similar pattern in each case, with learners travelling from the periphery of learning communities to becoming full participants and core members. Wenger later argued communities of practice are an integral part of our daily lives, 'so informal and so pervasive that they rarely come into explicit focus, but for the same reason they are also quite familiar' (Wenger 1998, p. 7). Communities of practice are part of lived experience, so commonplace that they often go unobserved.

Wenger argues that learning is an unavoidable aspect of existence, that it is ongoing, and he makes a distinction between learning and teaching: 'Learning and teaching are not inherently linked. Much learning takes place without teaching, and indeed much teaching takes place without learning' (p. 267). Similarly, Lave (2009) writes, 'It is difficult, when looking closely at everyday activity, to avoid the conclusion that learning is ubiquitous in ongoing activity, though often unrecognized as such' (p. 201). Intentional instruction, therefore, is not the sole source or necessary cause of learning. Recognizing that learning is not contained in a classroom, we also recognize how technology can facilitate effective learning irrespective of the learner's location, a point noted by Lave and Wenger (1991) who argue that a community of practice does not necessarily imply co-presence (p. 98). Gikas and Grant (2013) argue, 'learning occurs wherever a learner is and is not tied to a *space* inside a brick and mortar building or even confined to a *space* inside an online course management system. Learning happens regardless of location' (p. 24). It is not a question of whether technologies can facilitate effective learning and teaching, but of how technology can do it, both inside and outside classrooms.

Wenger (1998) defines a community of practice as, 'the sustained pursuit of a shared enterprise' (p. 45) characterized by mutually intelligible practices, evolving over time (Wenger et al. 2009, p. 56). It is a useful definition within a higher education context because students will commonly (though far from exclusively) be on a learning journey of three years' duration, supported by lecturers, student services and institutional policies. Furthermore, it is practice that gives the community coherence (Wenger 1998, p. 49); the successful outcome of the student's learning journey is the result of a sustained pursuit within a higher education community of practice. Therefore, and in common with Disruptive Innovation, practice is primary.

In addition, Wenger (1998) writes of 'a shared repertoire of ways of doing things' (p. 49) as a defining feature of a community of practice. The use of repertoire suggests rehearsed practice and also stresses performance and engagement, thus creating possibilities for innovation as individual

human subjects collaborate. Bueger (2013) states that repertoire in a community of practice 'is also comprised of symbols and gestures, language
tools and concepts' (p. 1816), thus implying a link with Activity Theory, as
intertraffic between communities and tools in pursuit of objects develops
and consolidates identity. The shared enterprise, the sustained pursuit, is
mediated through tools.

IDENTITY

The Community of Practice challenges established theories of learning:
'Conventional explanations view learning as a process by which a learner
internalizes knowledge ... This focus on internalization ... suggests that
knowledge is largely cerebral, and takes the individual as the nonproblematic
unit of analysis' (Lave and Wenger 1991, p. 47). Subsequently, Wenger
(1998) writes about institutional learning as 'largely based on the assumption
that learning is an individual process, that is has a beginning and an end, that
it is best separated from the rest of our activities, and that it is the result of
teaching' (p. 3). Instead of accepting these starting points, the Community of
Practice theory centres on identity formation in social contexts, arguing that
learning is a question of developing an identity through practice, as the
learner moves inwards from the periphery. Learning is therefore necessarily
social, involving interaction with other community members. In this sense,
there is a link between the Community of Practice and Activity Theory, as
identity is seen as an evolving practice rather than a fixed entity. Moreover,
the Community of Practice theory highlights the relationship between the
subject and the community.

   Lave and Wenger (1991) argue that the person is 'a newcomer becoming
an old-timer, whose changing knowledge, skill, and discourse are part of a
developing identity – in short, a member of a community of practice'
(p. 122). Identity is in a state of flux in the community of practice, steered
by the context in which the identity is being formed and the centre towards
which it moves, similar to how identity is understood in Activity Theory
(Vygotsky 1930; Leontiev 1978) as the subject pursues the object. However, while Activity Theory stresses identity as a construct, it also identifies
the subject (the individual) as a distinct node in an activity system, whereas
the role of the individual in the community of practice is more fluid, as
identity develops in the subject's movement from the periphery to the
centre.

In common with Activity Theory, the Community of Practice theory views identity as something that can be redefined rather than an essential quality, underlining the point that the Community of Practice views learning as fundamentally social; identity is not hermetic but is constituted socially. That said, Wenger (1998) later adds complexity to the position by stating, 'The concept of identity serves as a pivot between the social and the individual ... it is the social, the cultural, the historical with a human face' (p. 145). He develops his argument by stating, 'Identity is not some primordial core of personality that already exists. Nor is it something we acquire at some point in the same way that, at a certain age, we grow a set of permanent teeth ... our identity is something we constantly renegotiate during the course of our lives' (pp. 154–155). As Fenton-O'Creevey et al. (2014) argue, 'identity is not just an individual attribute, but is negotiated anew in each community we participate in' (p. 33), a point echoing Wenger's (1998) earlier claim that 'all learning eventually gains its significance in the kind of person we become' (p. 226). Individuals adjust and adapt to find an accommodation within the overall community identity, and the community identity can, similarly, be redefined through the practice of individuals. In common with Activity Theory, there is interaction between elements; the subject and community influence each other.

Wenger (1998) argues, 'Because learning transforms who we are and what we can do, it is an experience of identity. It is ... a process of becoming' (p. 215). If learning is a matter of becoming, of attaining an identity, then the study of learning centres on paying attention to the process of becoming. Therefore, when technological skills are acquired, it is in pursuit of an identity in a community of practice sense, as well as a defined object in an Activity Theory sense. This argument forms a distinction between the Community of Practice and Disruptive Innovation, as the latter views the use of technologies in more utilitarian terms of getting jobs done, though it could equally be argued that the construction of an identity is itself a task, and many practices within a community are about getting a job done. Constructing a successful, working identity is central in a community of practice.

The use of disruptive technologies in higher education can support the construction of a student identity although, crucially, it can also support the construction of different identities to suit different contexts. Wenger et al. (2009) argue, 'increasingly, individuals are not members of only one community; they belong to a substantial number of communities, teams, and networks – active in some, less so in others' (p. 58), while Wenger (1998) argues, 'we belong to several communities of practice at any given time. And the communities of practice to which we belong change over the course of our lives' (p. 6). Subjects construct different identities in different contexts, suggesting we can think of communities of practice as we think of the more sophisticated understandings of Activity Theory, with different systems interacting and overlapping with each other, and with tension and contradiction occurring both within and between systems and communities.

Identity is a starting point for the Community of Practice theory in the same way that the subject can be the starting point for an Activity Theory analysis (but so can the intertraffic between subject and object, or, and most commonly, the identification of the object). Identity is a resource in learning and teaching but it is not static; one of the accomplishments, though also dangers, of education can be to steer identity. Education therefore entails significant responsibility; Wenger (1998) argues, 'Education ... concerns the opening of identities – exploring new ways of being that lie beyond our current state' (p. 263). Vygotsky (1930), too, recognizes the transformative potential of education; if identity is constructed, education can influence the identity to which the learner aspires. The process of education can, if planned and managed benignly, construct an informed and self-reflective identity, as new and innovative forms of practice are made visible and move out of the hidden curriculum.

LEGITIMATE PERIPHERAL PARTICIPATION

Lave and Wenger (1991) identify legitimate peripheral participation, their term for the learning undertaken by newcomers to a community of practice, as a means of understanding learning (p. 40). Learners enter communities as newcomers or as apprentices or as undergraduate students, but replete with prior histories which influence how they interact with their new environment: prior history is also one of the factors influencing how the newcomer is treated by established members of the community. The idea of the individual subject as collage or palimpsest underlines the argument that the newcomer is always potentially disruptive and innovative, because of the experiences and practices they bring with them.

Kogut and Metiu (2001) argue that the internet software community is characterized by legitimate peripheral participation in its apprentice stage (p. 251), as new community members strive to demonstrate their competence to old hands, though the open source software community is somewhat different from mainstream organizations in this regard as it has no clear and definite owner (Nagy et al. 2016). The centre is not always easily identifiable in a community of practice, especially when that community is online, without a tangible, physical presence.

Wenger-Trayner and Wenger-Trayner (2014) argue, 'When newcomers are entering a community, it is mostly the regime of competence that is pulling and transforming their experience – until their experience reflects the competence of the community . . . Conversely, experience can also pull, challenge, and transform the community's regime of competence. A member can find a new solution to a problem and attempt to convince the community it is better than existing practice' (p. 14). The Community of Practice overlaps with Activity Theory here, too, as subjects can influence their communities as well as being influenced by them. For example, students enter university virtual learning environments and other institutional resources as peripheral participants and can be encouraged to engage more fully with the learning community and become a full participant, though they can also be discouraged through practices that exclude. Wenger (1998) argues that interaction between newcomers and old-timers should be encouraged, thus potentially aiding the community of practice's common purpose and creating the conditions in which movement from the periphery to the centre is smoother, as well as creating the conditions in which the community itself can change and innovate, though the latter process can pose a challenge to the community.

Students starting at university as legitimate peripheral participants acquire, over time, the identity of a student, a process arguably as important as the acquisition of subject knowledge and indeed a necessary process sitting alongside the inculcation of subject knowledge. New students are able to model their future identity on the practices of established members of the student community and may learn about disruptive technologies and the purposes, educational or social, to which they are put by more experienced students, though, and perhaps more commonly, new entrants to a community can be bearers of disruptive technologies and Disruptive Innovation. Informal learning communities can be as influential as the formal curriculum; the construction of student identity is steered by a range of both institutional and non-institutional factors. Legitimate peripheral participation is a vital stage in the construction of an identity and a spawning ground for innovation.

Newcomers can acquire practices which already prevail informally within the existing community, even if the practices contradict an official, institutional edict. Wenger (1998) notes, 'newcomers are no fools: once they have actual access to the practice, they soon find out what counts' (p. 155). In education, there is a contradiction between institutional policies and the curriculum on the one hand, and actual, quotidian practice on the other (what we might think of as the hidden curriculum) but, and in line with Activity Theory and expansive learning, the contradiction can give rise to innovation and enhancement if the university is willing to engage constructively with the disruptive technology practices of students and, for that matter, lecturers. The object of the higher education activity system, successful experiences and outcomes, does not change, but practices to that end change because of technology, and it is for universities to recognize and seek to reconcile the gap between technology policies and technology practice, by accepting the widespread use of disruptive technologies.

Certain individuals, generally on the periphery of a higher education community of practice, function as brokers, defined by Wenger (1998) as 'people who can introduce elements of one practice into another' (p. 105). The question is one of whether universities engage constructively with disruptive technologies introduced by brokers, or retreat into a closed space supported by institutional technologies only. The latter strategy has the advantage of constructing a clear institutional identity and creating a demarcation between the university and the outside world, but it is a limiting identity and imposes practices which may not be conducive to getting jobs done. Wenger (1998) identifies how 'Joining a community of practice involves entering not only its internal configuration but also its relations with the rest of the world' (p. 103) and, in the context of a university, the institution cannot control the external relations created and maintained by its students and lecturers. A university seeking to direct technology enhanced learning will benefit from recognizing the existing and emerging practices of its students and lecturers, in order to have relevant strategies that students and lecturers will find credible and workable in practice.

Lave and Wenger (1991) had previously discussed power relations in a community of practice: 'As a place in which one moves toward more-intensive participation, peripherality is an empowering position. As a place in which one is kept from participating more fully – often legitimately . . . it is a disempowering position' (p. 36). More recently (Farnsworth et al. 2016), Wenger has argued that the Community of Practice is 'a profoundly political theory of learning . . . learning always implies power relations' (p. 151). A university's strategy regarding technology enhanced learning may influence whether a student feels empowered or disenfranchised, depending on whether the student's informal learning practices are encouraged or discouraged on an institutional level (technology enhanced learning strategies are considered in Chap. 5). The use of Bring Your Own Device (BYOD), for example, can lead to feelings of student empowerment if students are using technologies they own and know how to use effectively. Practices not influenced by the institution may be most prevalent at the periphery, and thus the periphery may be a place where innovation is most apparent; Wenger (Farnsworth et al. 2016) states, 'from an innovation perspective you may want to include the perspective of a newcomer who has a naïve view of things and who is not stuck in history. Power can prevent learning by silencing voices' (p. 154). Wenger (1998) talks about the 'wisdom of peripherality' (p. 216); the newcomer is an obvious candidate for innovator, precisely because the newcomer is not steeped in existing practices, but innovation can often be conflated with transgression of community norms and thus innovation can threaten both the division of labour and, more tellingly, the distribution of power in a community. Fenton-O'Creevey et al. (2014) acknowledge the disruptive potential of innovation at the periphery: 'If we seek to enable and enrich cross-boundary learning we should start from the explicit acknowledgement that it involves experiences of failure, challenges to your sense of who you are, even sometimes abandoning cherished beliefs and values' (p. 2). The periphery can readily be the locus of innovation, but innovation can be an uncomfortable process. Subjects who cross boundaries enact practices which may enhance but also threaten the new community, the new activity system that they enter.

Learning Design

Wenger (1998) argues that learning is controlled by the learning community, not by the external drivers that prompted the formation of the learning community and adds, 'Learning cannot be designed. Ultimately, it belongs to the realm of experience and practice' (p. 225). He later argues that learning is a matter of imagination and, 'In a world that is not predictable, improvisation and innovation are more than desirable, they are essential' (pp. 227, 233), concluding, 'No community can fully design the learning of another ... No community can fully design its own learning' (p. 234). Learning eludes institutional boundaries and it is for institutions to recognize learning rather than to limit it by edict. As Wenger-Trayner and Wenger-Trayner (2014) argue, 'A mandate or a set of standards may give rise to a practice, but they do not produce the practice; the practitioners do'

(p. 16). Identifying practice as foundational connects the Community of Practice theory with Disruptive Innovation, and recognizing that innovation is essential connects the community of practice with Activity Theory and expansive learning, because innovation ensures activity systems are not static.

Wenger (1998) describes design figuratively as, 'a stake in the ground ... It must set up a framework, but it depends on this framework being negotiable in practice' (p. 235). Therefore, learning for Wenger is a creative process, the outcomes of which cannot be determined absolutely. Wenger's argument can also be linked to Engeström's expansive learning (1987), and Vygotsky's argument for play as a form of learning (1930), because learning relies on creativity and improvisation. Practice strays beyond design into its own, socially negotiated space. Wenger argues, 'The first requirement of educational design is to offer opportunities for engagement' (p. 271), but once engagement is, rightly, present, the original design is up for renegotiation and the outcomes of the learning are no longer predictable.

Wenger (1998) argues, 'practice cannot be the result of design, but instead constitutes a response to design' (p. 233). Institutions may lay out the form they intend learning to take, but actual learning is more unpredictable and has the inherent potential to be disruptive: 'One can attempt to institutionalize a community of practice, but the community of practice itself will slip through the cracks and remain distinct from its institutionalization' (p. 229). Hence, 'Institutionalization ... has a limited ability to mobilize the power of practice' (p. 243). Learning has a formal trajectory, especially in the context of assessed programmes at universities, but there is no institutional fetter on learning, as learning can take different forms, especially as contradictions within communities of practice or activity systems become apparent. The formal community of practice can attempt to restrict the informal community of practice but, in so doing, it will become separated from learning as an emerging process. Learning as a practice is open to disruption.

COMMUNITY OF PRACTICE: COMMENTARY AND CRITIQUE

Fuller and Unwin (2004) argue the roles of newcomer and expert are not stable within the Community of Practice; novices can be more adept than experts at some tasks, for example, those relying on technology. Power relations, however, are a key factor. If the experts engage in dialogue with adept novices, the community as a whole benefits, but the role of expert may need to be reconfigured. Alternatively, experts can assert their power by excluding the expertise of novices; novices can use technologies to support learning, but experts can deem those technologies inadmissible. Wenger-Trayner and Wenger-Trayner (2014) argue, 'A challenge or a claim to competence may be refused by the community; a newcomer may be marginalized' (p. 15). Regarding the practices of newcomers as legitimate opens up the community to the possibility of innovation, but Fuller and Unwin (2004) present the possibility that a human subject can be both a newcomer and an expert in the same community. Whether a new technology is a passport or an impediment to entry depends primarily on the community gatekeepers who, in the case of universities, are likely to be the teaching faculty (Anderson and McCune 2013).

Jewson (2007b) writes about individuals on the outskirts: 'Those on the periphery of a network may have attenuated connections with the centres of decision making but nevertheless exercise great importance as the primary point of contact with outsiders and members of other networks' (p. 73). Jewson gives physical examples (receptionists, concierges) but the online world is relevant, too. A newcomer to a university can bring with them a technology they have used beforehand, thereby potentially linking their new community to other networks. Technologies are well suited to Wenger's wisdom of peripherality (1998, p. 216) because of their potential to change practice. Moreover, linking a community to other communities opens up the possibility of boundary-crossing, which can accelerate innovation.

Jewson (2007a) explores the formation of identities within a community of practice. He acknowledges the importance of virtual environments but his argument takes a different focus: 'A major shift is occurring in the physical spaces of work alongside the emergence of virtual work space' (p. 160). Jewson suggests that the panopticon (a central position from which all activity can be observed by those in charge) is replaced by the polyopticon, where everyone is able to see everyone else in open plan offices, or rooms full of desktop computers in universities. Jewson argues that the underlying design vision is 'intended to foster serendipitous cross-fertilization of thoughts and perspectives' (p. 163) but it can also comprise policing, as can the data and learning analytics to which universities have potential access.

Networking in universities and other workplaces is a near-unavoidable consequence of inhabiting the same place. Within this framework 'performance of personality' becomes a key career asset (Jewson 2007a, p. 164). Jewson suggests individuals have to have 'a chameleon-like quality ...

moving into and out of quite different ways of behaving' (p. 167), linking with the idea that individual human subjects exist within a series of communities of practice (or as members of activity systems) and that the subject is not static but is constructed anew in each context. Individuals produce and develop different identities, both learning and social, supported by different technologies; demarcation of technology use is consequently an appropriate strategy to develop and serve different identities. Moreover, online identities can be aspirational more than they are authentic, exposing issues inherent in the performance of personality.

Different practices are supported by different technologies in pursuit of different objects (in an Activity Theory sense) and in support of different identities in a community of practice sense. More broadly, if distinctions between the individual and the collective are problematic, as Wenger argues (1998, p. 141), open plan spaces are not necessary for cross-fertilization and may be more about creating, intentionally or not, a polyopticon than they are about generating a creative learning or work space. Not only is physical co-presence not necessary for innovation, it may, in the context of highly scrutinized workplaces, be an impediment to innovation, as individual subjects feel under pressure to conform. In technology enhanced learning, the use of BYOD frees users from direct observation, though data analytics can still enable surveillance of users' practices, comprising a twenty-first century panopticon. That said, BYOD also changes the dynamics of learning and teaching, creating a sovereign state, in relation to the university, for the individual user, as they own the hardware.

Nickson et al. (2003) examine barriers to entry to a community, before the individual can be considered a peripheral participant. The authors' focus is the service industry and the idea that applicants have to hold particular persona attributes before they can be allowed entrance to the community. More specifically, they see social class as a key factor: 'Students who have access to higher education, in particular, may undergo a process of socialisation that allows them to further refine and develop the cultural capital which may be inherent anyway from their largely middle-class backgrounds' (p. 194). Conversely, as Wenger (1998) argues, 'When institutionally marginalized students leave school, taking institutionally marginalized jobs ... fits in with what they have learned in school. It merely extends the trajectory and institutional identity that schooling has offered them.' (p. 270). From this perspective, technology usage is influenced socio-economically along the lines suggested by Hargittai (2002, 2010), implying a level of analysis not accounted for explicitly in the second generation activity system but implicit in the Community of Practice theory which recognizes that newcomers are expected to adjust to the identity of the community. Moreover, a core tenet of Disruptive Innovation is that innovation makes goods or services available to communities who had not had access to them before, but it neglects to analyse fully how barriers to technology adoption may be cultural as well as economic. If the identity of the community is, in effect, a foreign language to some newcomers, they are at a structural disadvantage. Universities have entry requirements which play a role in determining the type of newcomer to the community of practice; universities can have, in effect, an identity test for entrance as well as an academic threshold.

Unwin (2007) identifies a tension in the Community of Practice theory: 'the survival and reproduction of communities of practice depends on newcomers but, at the same time, their arrival threatens the role of old-timers' (p. 112). A similar point was made by Lave and Wenger (1991) who state, 'there is a fundamental contradiction in the meaning to newcomers and old-timers of increasing participation by the former; for the centripetal development of full participants, and with it the successful production of a community of practice, also implies the *replacement* of old-timers' (p. 149, emphasis in original). From a more conservative position, Lea (in, Barton and Tusting 2005) states, 'it could be argued that most university teaching and learning practices are not about inclusion but tend to position undergraduate students as permanent novices, never attaining full membership of an academic community of practice' (p. 193). Looking at the exclusive nature of communities, and at the effects of marginalization and exclusion, we can start to understand rebellion as a structural feature of communities of practice, a mode of expression for those marginalized by the dominant discourse. However, Wenger (1998) argues, 'As a form of participation, rebellion often reveals a greater commitment that does passive conformity' (p. 77) and, from an Activity Theory perspective, Roth and Lee (2007) argue, 'a child who insists on creative acts of rebellion during instruction time is as much a constitutive member of the classroom and its collective identity as another who is a model student' (p. 216). Tension is inscribed in communities of practice and is not necessarily indicative of a failing community. Moreover, subjects can remain on the periphery by choice if that position fulfils their needs, such as a student concerned only with learning for the assessment rather than deep learning, a strategic and conscious decision which may allow them to enter another community of practice (such as a place of work) to which they feel more committed.

Communities of Practice learning, therefore, is not smoothly centripetal, as Wenger (1998) states: 'Because the term "community" is usually a very positive one, I cannot emphasize enough that these interrelations arise out of engagement in practice and not out of an idealized view of what a community should be like' (p. 77). Wenger also stresses that communities of practice 'are not havens of peace' (p. 101) and goes further by arguing, 'communities of practice should not be romanticized; they can reproduce counterproductive patterns, injustices, prejudices, racism, sexism, and abuses of all kinds. In fact, I would argue that they are the very locus of such reproduction' (p. 132). The Community of Practice theory has been applied to identify internal rationalizations of their conduct by Somali pirates (Bueger 2013) and to the linguistic practices, and the exploitative power relations these practices illuminate, in a community of street-level sex workers (Read 2014). In each case, violence is justified by the internal values and practices of the community of practice, values and practices that reflect the distribution and concentration of power in those communities. Communities of practice are structurally similar to one another but are radically dissimilar in their individual, internal practices. Newcomers bring new practices, including with technologies, and the community has to decide whether to accommodate or exclude. The community's decision can enhance or ossify its own life. Institutions place parameters on what is considered acceptable as learning. Linking with Activity Theory, and in order for learning to become expansive, tension is essential and thus the community of practice has to have tension within it in order to be a viable, ongoing community with the potential to renew, reform and revivify itself.

THE COMMUNITY OF PRACTICE AND ACTIVITY THEORY

The Community of Practice has similarities with Engeström's second generation activity system, in the sense that the activity system identifies the community as a node and the Community of Practice theory examines the nature and composition of the community. Wenger (1998) describes communities of practice as 'nodes of communication' (p. 252) and identifies a community of practice as, 'a point of entry into a broader conceptual framework of which it is a constitutive element' (p. 5), a definition which aligns the community of practice with the activity system's community node. A community of practice is less distinct in its own component parts and practices than an activity system, though it feeds into an activity system. The community is the point of entry for the subject, who may not have been active in the formation of the object and, in the case of a student entering a university, is joining a system in which the object of successfully completing a programme is preordained.

There are clearly distinctions between a community of practice and an activity system, as a community of practice implies a relatively stable centre towards which the learner moves, whereas activity systems as understood by Engeström strive towards the construction of new objects through expansive learning, but there are overlaps between the theories, too, such as the subject as a construct and the deterministic influence of community. Examining the community of practice alongside Activity Theory is useful because Activity Theory identifies specific social factors influencing the individual subject, and the community of practice traces a subject's development within a community. Moreover, Roth and Lee (2007) argue, 'During the pursuit of the object, subjects not only produce outcomes but also produce/reproduce themselves ... Identity is evidently a dialectical feature: It is continuously produced and reproduced in practical activity' (p. 215). Activity Theory therefore links with the Community of Practice argument that learning is about the construction of an identity. In addition, tension is implicit in the construction of a new identity; both Activity Theory and the Community of Practice depend upon tension to fuel change and innovation.

Lave and Wenger (1991) recognize that communities of practice are not isolated or impermeable; they exist 'in relation with other tangential and overlapping communities of practice' (p. 98). Wenger (1998) writes of constellations of practice which share members and artefacts, and later writes: 'Some communities need to constantly interact with other communities to form broader constellations and networks' (Wenger et al. 2009, p. 97). Communities of practice overlap with other communities of practice, as activity systems overlap. The interaction between activity systems exposes the possibility for contradictions, and thus the possibility of expansive learning, as practices and technologies from different systems cross borders and interact. Similarly, contradictions between overlapping communities of practice are, themselves, worth studying as potential cases of Disruptive Innovation. The Community of Practice and Activity Theory are both interested in change over time, in systems which are not static and which interact with other communities and systems, in potentially innovative forms of boundary-crossing.

In common with activity systems, communities of practice develop, their existence sustained by factors including the community's participants. Hence, argues Wenger, 'The enterprise is never fully determined by an outside mandate, by a prescription, or by any individual participant. Even when a community of practice arises in response to some outside mandate, the practice evolves into the community's own response to that mandate' (p. 80). A community of practice is always in motion (Lave and Wenger 1991, p. 123). In common with second generation Activity Theory and expansive learning, therefore, the Community of Practice sees the community as febrile, prone to internal contradiction and change, though, and paradoxically, with a centre of gravity and expertise. Within expansive learning, the object, the Activity Theory equivalent of the community of practice's centre, is reimagined and redefined as a consequence of expansive learning. Reformulation of the object is the point of expansive learning whereas, in the Community of Practice, the subject moves towards an identifiable centre which is less precarious than the activity system's object.

Engeström and Miettenen's (1999) perspective on the connections between the community of practice and Activity Theory stresses the limitations of the former: 'The theory of legitimate peripheral participation depicts learning and development primarily as a one-way movement from the periphery, occupied by novices, to the center, inhabited by experienced masters of the given practice. What seems to be missing is movement outward and in unexpected directions: questioning of authority, criticism, innovation, initiation of change' (p. 12). Reconfiguring, for a moment, the second generation Activity Theory triangle as a circle (a suitable figure for a community of practice), the Activity Theory object can comprise the community of practice centre. However, in expansive learning, the object (the centre, in this instance) is redefined, and thus the community has no stable centre but, instead, a centre that can change its own identity in the presence of contradictions emanating from innovation at the periphery. To imagine a snapshot of Activity Theory reconfigured as a community of practice, the subject on the periphery travels towards the object at the centre, using tools to enable the movement. The rules of the community will dictate the behavioural codes of the community and the division of labour will determine the subject's role. In order for innovation to happen, however, the subject will need to challenge the boundaries created by the rules and the division of labour. Substantial innovation is therefore necessarily disruptive; sustaining innovation can make the community function more smoothly (similar to Activity Theory when it understands rather than resolves contradictions) but Disruptive Innovation has to change the community's practice fundamentally and redefine its centre.

Additional complexities arise in communities of practice when they are monetized. A case study by Pohjola and Puusa (2016) shows what happened when an online community of practice (focused on a community of enthusiasts sharing plans for converting petrol and diesel to electric cars) attracted an outside investor. Two main changes occurred: 'the expectations and demand to obtain results increased, and the need for monitoring and reporting emerged' (p. 476). This case study is analogous to higher education and the move towards the individual increasingly bearing the costs through tuition fees. With the monetization and privatization of higher education, expectations of successful outcomes become more pronounced and an audit culture intensifies. The emergence of the Teaching Excellence Framework in UK higher education, for example, may be seen as a byproduct of a monetized system, adding to the Research Excellence Framework and the National Student Survey in the intensification of an audit culture. Monetization provides a good example of how communities of practice are not hermetically sealed and are, instead, influenced by wider social and economic practices.

Engeström sees contradiction as the catalyst for expansive learning, but the problem is more structural and intractable for Lave and Wenger (1991). Wenger (1998) tries to address the contradiction between institutionalization and practice: 'Designing processes and policies is important, but in the end it is practice that produces results, not the processes and policies. The challenge is to support rather than displace the knowledgeability of practice' (pp. 243–244). Institutional communities of practice need to be flexible enough to allow for innovation. Moreover, innovation in itself may be a response to outside pressures from other communities of practice, but innovation has the potential to replenish and revivify the community of practice. The knowledgeability of practice can enhance, not threaten, the institution. Tension can fuel and empower and does not necessarily require a resolution but, instead, accommodation and understanding.

CONCLUSION

The Community of Practice identifies a range of stakeholders, both peripheral and central, contributing to learning and teaching generally and, within the context of this book, in higher education communities specifically, focusing on technology enhanced learning. This book interprets the community node in an activity system as a community of practice.

Lave and Wenger (1991) identify a tension between continuity and displacement as a fundamental feature of learning (pp. 114 and 123). In this sense, their work is more closely aligned with Christensen, but whereas Lave and Wenger see the tension as a structural feature of a community of practice, Christensen reads the tension as a symptom of the emergence of a disruption, with the resolution of the tension being weighted in the disruption's favour if the product, service or practice it offers to users is simpler, cheaper and more convenient than that of its incumbent rival.

Christensen and Engeström are alike in seeing disruption as an opportunity for progress. Contrastingly, Wenger (1998) acknowledges disruption but stresses continuity: 'Destabilizing events do take place, but communities of practice reorganize their histories around them, developing specific responses to them that honor the continuity of their learning' (p. 98), thus implying more stability than is available within Activity Theory, which places the redefinition of the object, the centre, as an historically necessary consequence of expansive learning. Communities of practice are not infinite but they do have the capability to endure for as long as they fulfil a purpose useful to their members, a view which bodes well for the traditional university.

Wenger et al. (2009) have more in common with Disruptive Innovation when they stress factors conducive to technology adoption: 'Simplicity is a real plus, especially at the beginning when commitment to the community can be tentative' (p. 116). Simple technologies can facilitate smooth entry into a community of practice, enabling newcomers to move more easily from the periphery to the centre. Wenger et al.'s (2009) recommendation is explicit: 'No matter what goodies you find in your scanning of the technology landscape, focus on the simplest structure you can get away with at the beginning . . . From there you can incrementally add, subtract, and adjust your tools based on their use by the community' (p. 132).

Students and lecturers utilize specific technologies for specific jobs, supporting their learning and personal identities. Certain technologies (for example, Wikipedia) may have a less impressive academic veneer than others, but they get used, primarily because of their simplicity, convenience and ease of use; Knight and Pryke (2012), in a study at Liverpool Hope University found both students and lecturers making widespread use of Wikipedia (75% of the sample) and found that 'ease of access' (p. 649) was a factor influencing the choice of Wikipedia, in line with Christensen's definition of disruptive technologies. Disruptive technologies facilitate inculcation in communities of practice, yet communities of practice also engage in intertraffic with technologies and with social factors in an activity system sense, pursuing objects and encountering tensions and contradictions. The newcomer to a higher education community of practice may use Wikipedia but come to understand that it is not approved of. The newcomer may therefore have to stop using Wikipedia or, and more probably, conceal their use of it. Adherence to the community's rules can be purely nominal and can be contradicted by practice.

It is possible to interpret Wikipedia, a disruptive technology, as a community of practice. The bulk of users are at the periphery, taking what they want from the resource without feeling the need to join the core of contributors. In this sense, Wikipedia illustrates the principle that movement from the periphery to the centre is not inevitable; individual subjects may choose to remain at the periphery if what they do there enables them to get jobs done. As Wenger's (1998) research was in a workplace, the use of Wikipedia is analogous to the employee who does not wish to progress within the organization but uses the job for wages to support other aspects of their life; in each case, the subject has a utilitarian relationship with the community. It is also possible to consider the Wikipedia community of practice in relation to the university community of practice. As membership of the former may not align with the practices and values of the latter (such as the role of the acknowledged expert), tension may arise between the two communities. That tension can either be repressed or surfaced but, in the case of Wikipedia, surfacing the tension may involve the university community of practice being willing to sanction practices which do not align with entrenched conventions, but which recognize that users want simple, convenient and free access to information in support of their learning. Linking the community of practice to Christensen and Raynor (2003), Wikipedia is something that users hire to get jobs done. Pleasingly, from the user's point of view, it is free to use, and simple and convenient.

Tensions arise in a community of practice between the formal parameters of the institution and the practice of community members. Wenger argues, 'The point of design for learning is to make organizations ready for the emergent by serving the inventiveness of practice and the potential for innovation inherent in its emergent structure' (1998, p. 245). A key task in a community of practice, therefore, is to navigate the contradiction between design and practice, suggestive of the procedure of Activity Theory. In this sense, Wenger's stress on continuity in a community of practice gets superseded by a model of organizational development which is more in line with Engeström's expansive learning, especially in the controlled (albeit limited) sense suggested by Avis (2007, 2009), as organizations renew themselves through the management of a contradiction which threatens to disrupt existing practices. Design and practice are in a state of tension in a community of practice; practice cannot be contained within the parameters of design because it is always in some stage of development as newcomers arrive at the community's periphery with the potential to innovate.

The response of universities to the disruptive usage of technologies is a key determinant of technology adoption. The reactionary approach on the part of universities is to prohibit the use of disruptive technologies, but this is directly consequential for learning and teaching: 'Denying access and limiting the centripetal movement of newcomers and other practitioners changes the learning curriculum' (Lave and Wenger 1991, p. 123). The alternative is for universities to engage constructively with disruptive technologies, but in a community of practice this may require rethinking the power relations between the centre and the periphery.

Ultimately, Wenger et al. (2009) offer an optimistic analysis of technology usage in communities of practice: 'Viewed as a trend, the history of mutual influence between technology and community creates a vortex of inventiveness that propels both forward' (p. 172). Practice with technology entails the potential for organizational change. Change is not necessarily for the better, but stasis in higher education is inevitably ossification, because wider social and economic contexts are not static.

The university is a historically resilient model for learning and teaching but it depends upon innovation, even though it does not always welcome innovation. Technology usage in a community of practice, especially at the community's periphery, can result in new and interesting identities for communities, perhaps also redefining what expertise in that community looks like.

This chapter has used the Community of Practice theory to more fully define the community node in an activity system and to analyse the links between communities, technologies and innovation. The chapter has disavowed the digital natives hypothesis (Prensky 2001), but confirms the importance of practice, which can contradict institutional edict but, in so doing, can catalyse innovation.

The next and final chapter aims to synthesize the three theoretical perspectives of Disruptive Innovation, Activity Theory and the Community of Practice, in order to consider what action the higher education sector might take in response to disruptive technologies and Disruptive Innovation.

REFERENCES

Anderson, C., & McCune, V. (2013). Fostering meaning: Fostering community. *Higher Education, 66,* 283–296.

Avis, J. (2007). Engeström's version of activity theory: A conservative praxis? *Journal of Education and Work, 20*(3), 161–177.

Avis, J. (2009). Transformation or transformism: Engeström's version of activity theory? *Educational Review, 61*(2), 151–165.

Barton, D., & Tusting, K. (Eds.). (2005). *Beyond communities of practice: Language, power and social context.* Cambridge: Cambridge University Press.

Bennett, S., Maton, K., & Kervin, L. (2008). The "digital natives" debate: A critical review of the evidence. *British Journal of Educational Technology, 39*(5), 775–786.

Bueger, C. (2013). Practice, pirates and coast guards: The grand narrative of Somali piracy. *Third World Quarterly, 34*(10), 1811–1827.

Christensen, C. M., & Raynor, M. E. (2003). *The innovator's solution: Creating and sustaining successful growth.* Boston: Harvard Business School Press.

Corrin, L., Bennett, S., & Lickyer, L. (2010). Digital natives: Everyday life versus academic study. In L. Dirckinck-Holmfeld, V. Hodgson, C. Jones, M. de Laat, D. McConnell, & T. Ryberg (Eds.), *Proceedings of the 7th international conference on networked learning.* Lancaster: Lancaster University.

Engeström, Y. (1987). *Learning by expanding: An activity-theoretical approach to developmental research.* Helsinki: Orienta-Konsultit Oy. Retrieved from http://lchc.ucsd.edu/MCA/Paper/Engestrom/expanding/toc.htm

Engeström, Y., & Miettenen, R. (1999). Introduction. In Y. Engeström, R. Miettenen, & R.-L. Punamäki (Eds.), *Perspectives on activity theory* (pp. 1–18). Cambridge: Cambridge University Press.

Farnsworth, V., Kleanthous, I., & Wenger-Trayner, E. (2016). Communities of practice as a social theory of learning: A conversation with Etienne Wenger. *British Journal of Educational Studies, 64*(2), 1–22, 139–160.

Fenton-O'Creevey, M., Dimitriadis, Y., & Scobie, G. (2014). Failure and resilience at boundaries: The emotional process of identity work. In E. Wenger-Trayner, M. Fenton-O'Creevey, S. Kutchinson, S. Kubiak, & B. Wenger-Trayner (Eds.), *Learning in landscapes of practice: Boundaries, identity and knowledgeability in practice-based learning* (pp. 33–42). London: Routledge.

Fuller, A., & Unwin, L. (2004). Young people as teachers and learners in the workplace: Challenging the novice-expert dichotomy. *International Journal of Training and Development, 8*(1), 31–41.

Gikas, J., & Grant, M. M. (2013). Mobile computing devices in higher education: Student perspectives on learning with cellphones, smartphones and social media. *Internet and Higher Education, 19,* 18–26.

Hargittai, E. (2002). Second level digital divide. *First Monday, 7*(4). Retrieved from http://firstmonday.org/htbin/cgiwrap/bin/ojs/index.php/fm/article/view/942/864

Hargittai, E. (2010). Digital na(t)ives? Variation in internet skills and uses among members of the "net generation". *Sociological Inquiry, 80*(1), 92–114.

Henderson, M., Selwyn, N., Finger, G., & Aston, R. (2015). Students' everyday engagement with digital technology in university: Exploring patterns of use and "usefulness". *Journal of Higher Education Policy and Management, 37*(3), 308–319.

Jewson, N. (2007a). Communities of practice in their place: Some implications of changes in the spatial location of work. In J. Hughes, N. Jewson, & L. Unwin (Eds.), *Communities of practice: Critical perspectives*. Abingdon: Routledge.

Jewson, N. (2007b). Cultivating network analysis: Rethinking the concept of "community" within communities of practice. In J. Hughes, N. Jewson, & L. Unwin (Eds.), *Communities of practice: Critical perspectives*. Abingdon: Routledge.

Jones, C., & Healing, G. (2010). Net generation students: Agency and choice and the new technologies. *Journal of Computer Assisted Learning, 26*, 344–356.

Knight, C., & Pryke, S. (2012). Wikipedia and the university, a case study. *Teaching in Higher Education, 17*(6), 649–659.

Kogut, B., & Metiu, A. (2001). Open-source software development and distributed innovation. *Oxford Review of Economic Policy, 17*(2), 248–269.

Lave, J. (2009). The practice of learning. In K. Illeris (Ed.), *Contemporary theories of learning: Learning theorists, in their own words* (pp. 200–208). London: Routledge.

Lave, J., & Wenger, E. (1991). *Situated learning: Legitimate peripheral participation*. Cambridge: Cambridge University Press.

Leontiev, A. N. (1978). *Activity, consciousness and personality* (trans. Hall, M.J.). Englewood Cliffs: Prentice Hall.

Margaryan, A., Littlejohn, A., & Vojt, G. (2011). Are digital natives a myth or reality? University students' use of digital technologies. *Computers and Education, 56*, 429–440.

Nagy, D., Schussler, J., & Dubinsky, A. (2016). Defining and identifying disruptive innovations. *Industrial Marketing Management, 57*, 119–126.

Nickson, D., Warhurst, C., Cullen, A. M., & Watt, A. (2003). Bringing in the excluded? Aesthetic labour, skills and training in the "new" economy. *Journal of Education and Work, 16*(2), 185–203.

Pohjola, I., & Puusa, A. (2016). Group dynamics and the role of ICT in the life cycle analysis of community of practice-based product development: A case study. *Journal of Knowledge Management, 20*(3), 465–483.

Prensky, M. (2001). Digital natives, digital immigrants. *On the Horizon, 9*(5). Retrieved from http://www.marcprensky.com/writing/prensky%20-%20digital%20natives,%20digital%20immigrants%20-%20part1.pdf

Read, K. W. (2014). Sex work: Constructing "families" with community of practice theory. *Community, Work and Family, 17*(1), 60–78.

Roth, W. M., & Lee, Y. J. (2007). "Vygotsky's neglected legacy": Cultural-historical activity theory. *Review of Educational Research, 77*(2), 186–232.

Selwyn, N. (2009). The digital native – Myth and reality. *Aslib Proceedings, 61*(4), 364–379.

Somyürek, S., & Coşkun, B. K. (2013). Digital competence: Is it innate talent of the new generation or an ability that must be developed? *British Journal of Educational Technology, 44*(5), E163–E166.

Unwin, L. (2007). English apprenticeship from past to present. In J. Hughes, N. Jewson, & L. Unwin (Eds.), *Communities of practice: Critical perspectives* (pp. 109–119). Abingdon: Routledge.

Vygotsky, L. (1930). The socialist alteration of man. In R. Van Der Veet & J. Valsiner (Eds.), *The Vygotsky reader* (pp. 175–184). Oxford: Blackwell.

Wenger, E. (1998). *Communities of practice: Learning, meaning, and identity.* Cambridge: Cambridge University Press.

Wenger, E., White, N., & Smith, J. D. (2009). *Digital habitats: Stewarding technology for communities.* Portland: CPsquare.

Wenger-Trayner, E., & Wenger-Trayner, B. (2014). Learning in a landscape of practice: A framework. In E. Wenger-Trayner, M. Fenton-O'Creevey, S. Kutchinson, S. Kubiak, & B. Wenger-Trayner (Eds.), *Learning in landscapes of practice: Boundaries, identity and knowledgeability in practice-based learning* (pp. 13–30). London: Routledge.

CHAPTER 5

Bidding the Waves Go Back: Engaging with Disruptive Innovation

INTRODUCTION

The previous chapter examined the Community of Practice theory and its relevance to Disruptive Technology Enhanced Learning. This final chapter synthesizes arguments from the previous three chapters on Disruptive Innovation, Activity Theory and the Community of Practice, leading to an overarching perspective on Disruptive Technology Enhanced Learning and on how disruptive technologies can be used to enhance learning and teaching. The chapter evaluates specific technologies, including Facebook, Massive Open Online Courses (MOOCs) and YouTube, and specific practices including Bring Your Own Device (BYOD) and learning analytics. The chapter also evaluates the predictive value of Disruptive Innovation and the presence of disruption in UK university strategies for technology enhanced learning. The chapter concludes with recommendations for enabling Disruptive Technology Enhanced Learning in higher education.

Disruptive technologies are used widely to support learning and teaching in higher education. This does not mean that students and lecturers are not using institutional, designed for learning technologies, but that their use of institutional technologies is in many cases secondary to their use of disruptive technologies. Furthermore, the technologies that are used by students and lecturers tend to conform to Christensen's core criteria (1997). This book therefore proposes a rethink of technology enhanced learning, rooted in students' and lecturers' practices.

© The Author(s) 2017
M. Flavin, *Disruptive Technology Enhanced Learning*,
DOI 10.1057/978-1-137-57284-4_5

111

Students' and lecturers' use of disruptive technologies has significant implications for higher education. For example, the practice of using Google and Wikipedia rather than institutional technologies has implications for the role of the university. Disruptive technologies have the potential to change aspects of higher education by providing quick and convenient access to knowledge resources; Eijkman (2010), in a study of Wikipedia, argues for 'a new knowledge economy which challenges the pre-eminent role of academia as the traditional gatekeeper to knowledge' (p. 181). Disruptive Technology Enhanced Learning also influences social relations in higher education, as disruptive technologies change practice and, as such, impact on higher education activity systems.

Universities can engage constructively with disruptive technologies by recognizing disruption as a product of practice and by recognizing the technologies used by students and lecturers to support learning and teaching. Universities can also engage constructively with disruptive technologies by recognizing the mismatch between the technologies they provide and the technologies students and lecturers use, and by rethinking their technology enhanced learning strategies in the light of practice; Karlsson (2014) asks the question, 'Should it [the university] continue to invest millions in making available information resources when free alternatives are consolidating their strength?' (pp. 1664–5). By undertaking an examination of technology use in higher education beginning with practice rather than with technologies, a more compelling narrative emerges to drive technology enhanced learning strategies at an institutional level.

In some respects, the enabling of disruptive technologies needs no prompting, as it is a core contention of Disruptive Innovation that disruption emerges from practice rather than design, and therefore disruption manages itself in the sense that it emerges from interactions between people and technologies; technologies are essentially inert until they become included in human practice. Furthermore, disruption needs no prompting within a second generation activity system, because contradictions accumulate structurally over time leading to new activity systems. Disruption, in the form of contradiction, is assured historically. However, institutional interventions can be made, enabling the disruptive use of technologies to be better accommodated within learning and teaching; Engeström (1999, p. 385) argues that deliberate intervention is usually required to achieve expansive learning. Moreover, disruption is commonplace in communities of practice as new entrants bring their own practices to a community, practices which morph to fit the community's existing norms but can also disrupt, challenge and change those norms. The periphery of a learning community is a prime site for innovation because it is where new, innovative technologies and practices often proliferate.

In an article in the *Harvard Business Review*, Christensen et al. (2015) summarize disruptive innovation. They write about it becoming a 'victim of its own success' and refer to the 'popularity of the initial formulation' (p. 46). However, this book argues that the simplicity of Disruptive Innovation is an asset; the theory lends itself to application across a range of practices, having been, for example, applied by Christensen and co-authors to education (2008) and higher education (2011). Disruptive Innovation, based on simple and easy to use disruptive technologies, is fundamentally easy to comprehend and easy to apply. Christensen et al. (2015) also argue, 'It is rare that a technology or product is inherently sustaining or disruptive,' reiterating that disruption is a matter of practice rather than design. A very similar point is made by Johnson et al. (2016) in relation to technology usage in the USA: 'While many of the technologies considered were not developed for the sole purpose of education, they have clear applications in the field' (p. 34). Technologies are not disruptive intrinsically but become disruptive through practice.

Disruptive technologies as a category resist easy reduction, unless we define disruptive technologies as technologies that are disruptive. The definition is less facile than it appears at first, because the emphasis in disruption is on practice, and it is the use of the technology that comprises the disruption (Flavin 2016b). From a Community of Practice perspective, Wenger et al. (2009) argue, 'the way communities use a tool can be different from what a designer intended... It is useful to find out how tools are really used' (p. 140), underlining the point that practice is primary, and further identifying purpose as a product of practice.

A disruptive technology acts as a tool in an activity system sense, its disruptiveness realized through practice and targeted at objects (in the sense of purposes). In order to develop along the lines argued for by Christensen, disruptive technologies need to attain a coterie of users and thus gain an effective foothold in markets. When users network, cross boundaries and collaborate, it creates the conditions in which disruptive technology use is more likely to be disseminated more widely. An effective academic community of practice can enable the dissemination through a community that encourages, rather than suppresses, innovation at its periphery. Aggregating these different perspectives and accepting disruption as a practice rather than an intention, Christensen's first definition of disruption is still the most useful, because it argues disruptive technologies are simpler, smaller, cheaper and more convenient than the incumbents they displace (1997, p. xv).

Disruptive technologies highlight the argument that knowledge is constructed and that learning is a collaborative practice, either explicitly so when learners work together or implicitly, even when the learner is nominally alone. As Wenger (1998) argues, 'Our knowing – even of the most unexceptional kind – is always too big, too rich, too ancient, and too connected for us to be the source of it individually' (p. 141). The point is underlined by Vygotsky (1930) and Leontiev (1977), who argue that consciousness itself is constructed historically and socially and therefore collaboratively. Knowledge is produced, and produced in contexts which are ultimately social. Disruptive technologies amplify this idea, showing how meaning arises from practice, as well as showing how existing practices influence emerging practices.

FACEBOOK

Previous research, as summarized by Manca and Ranieri (2013) suggests Facebook is used in education primarily to support social relationships and social capital (for example, Selwyn 2009; Ellison et al. 2011). That said, other studies summarized in Manca and Ranieri's account also show Facebook being used for more explicitly educational purposes, such as sharing notes (Bosch 2009; Fewkes and McCabe 2012). Furthermore, Amador and Amador (2014) show Facebook being used by an academic advisor to communicate with students, though the advisor was already known to most of the sample, suggesting relationships had been relocated rather than constructed through Facebook, and Tower et al. (2014) undertook a successful case study of Facebook being used to support learning on a Nursing programme in Australia.

Mazman and Usluel (2010) identify usefulness and ease of use as significant factors influencing the adoption of Facebook (p. 446), their study also being highlighted by Manca and Ranieri (2013, p. 490). The highlighting of ease of use links with the core definition of disruption offered by Christensen (1997, p. xv). Factors such as usefulness and ease of use correlate closely with Christensen's definition, suggesting that the conditions for a disruptive technology contribute to the likely adoption of Facebook and other social networking technologies for educational purposes.

The limited adoption of Facebook to support learning and teaching in higher education suggests students and lecturers practise technology demarcation; an interviewee of Salmon et al. (2015) described using Facebook to support a course as 'a little too intimate' (p. 10) and Hrastinski and Aghaee (2012) argue, based on interviews with students, 'Although all but one of the interviewed students use social media in their private lives, many of them are quite critical about using such media in education' (p. 458). Wang et al. (2012) studied the use of Facebook as a teaching tool, finding that students preferred it for social networking than for formal learning. In addition, Jones (2012) notes the distracting effect of social media technologies, whose automated processes (such as notifications) can pop up when students are working (p. 34). It may well be easier and more convenient for users to have separate technologies supporting their learning and their social lives, which does not mean that Facebook and other social media technologies are not used to support learning and teaching, but that social media technologies are likely to occupy a niche, and are less likely to comprise an effective front-end platform for learning and teaching (Flavin 2016b).

Timmis (2012) points out that students have a wealth of digital technologies available to them but is unclear whether this is an asset or a burden; a number of her interviewees employed a demarcation between technologies for study and technologies for social life (pp. 9–10). Furthermore, Hrastinski and Aghaee (2012) refer to digital dissonance, whereby relatively few students want to use social media technologies for explicitly learning tasks; their interviewees valued Facebook as a means of initiating communication but not as a tool for collaborative learning. Irwin et al. (2012), in an Australian context, created a Facebook page for a course but found only around half of the students stated it was effective and, moreover, students' usage of Facebook was similar to the use of a VLE, such as catching up on class content (p. 1227). In the USA, Camus et al. (2016) undertook a comparative study of student posts on Facebook and on a VLE, finding that the former was better suited to student participation and encouraging peer-to-peer dialogue, but the latter was better, 'for encouraging students to develop coherent arguments and apply course content in other contexts' (p. 84). One of the reasons for the limited pedagogical value of Facebook may be the nature of posts on Facebook, which can have a stream of consciousness quality (Rowe 2014, p. 242). The medium itself appears to be a significant determinant of the practice undertaken by users.

Facebook has the potential to be used disruptively; it enables easy networking and the location of individuals with similar study interests. However, this book argues that different technologies get used in pursuit of different objects, in the activity system sense of purposes. There is evidence of disruptive use of established technologies, with, for example, Google getting used in preference to academic journal aggregators such as Academic Search Complete, but established technologies are not necessarily prone to disruptive use. Instead, students and lecturers choose different technologies to undertake different tasks. The starting point is the identification of a job to be done and the selection of a technology tool to do the job (a choice underpinned by a range of factors, as this book has argued), an approach outlined by Christensen and Raynor (2003). Using a technology tool used ordinarily for socializing for, instead, learning and teaching can be problematic because it blurs lines that participants choose to maintain to get jobs done; Manca and Ranieri (2016) argue, 'Social media are playing a marginal role in academic life' (p. 229). Facebook has the potential to be a disruptive technology but it is not disruptive in practice on a large scale, and practice is the key determinant of disruption.

Massive Open Online Courses (MOOCs) and Virtual Worlds

The criteria for disruptive technologies can be applied to innovations in technology enhanced learning in higher education. For example, MOOCs have attracted interest in recent years; Diver and Martinez (2015) show that there was one published article on MOOCs in 2008, rising to 26 in 2012. MOOCs are free and they are convenient; they can be accessed from any networked device. They are also scalable; there is no limit to how many participants they can accommodate. Furthermore, MOOCs can potentially widen access to higher education, including to prestigious institutions, they can provide motivational content for pre-university students and they can provide materials to enable continuing professional development (Gordon 2014, p. 17). They can also enhance a university's brand recognition (Burd et al. 2015, p. 47).

Their simplicity, ease of use and cost are, however, more complex. Laurillard (2014) argues MOOCs are most suitable for learners who already have a grounding in the subject (she cites data claiming 85% of MOOC participants already have a degree), and other writers have drawn attention to the high dropout rates on MOOCs (for example, Yuan and Powell 2013; Diver and Martinez 2015; Ng'ambi 2015; Yang et al. 2015). One way to combat the high dropout rates for MOOCs is to communicate clearly the intended audience, an approach recommended by Liyanagunawardena et al. (2015) in a case study of a MOOC offered through the FutureLearn platform managed by the Open University in the UK, though targeting a specific audience may compromise the openness of MOOCs. Moreover, the fact that MOOCs are free to use belies the cost of MOOCs to institutions. For example, Gallagher and Garrett (2013) state Harvard and MIT invested 30 million dollars each in their MOOC collaboration, edX (p. 4). Furthermore, while MOOCs give greater access to the learning and teaching of universities, democratizing access to resources is not the same as access to education (Laurillard 2013).

Gordon (2014), using the metaphor of a journey on the Underground, states, 'MOOCs... may offer the scale and efficiency of the underground system and provide for the mass transport of individuals from start to finish. However, support within that system is limited and individuals can pass through the system with little context awareness, knowledge of what they are passing under or over, or engagement with others' (p. 14); a challenging question to emerge from the metaphor is whether it begins to articulate the undergraduate's overall learning journey, too, moving through a large and impersonal organization from fresher to graduate. MOOCs do not correspond to all of Christensen's core criteria and are not a disruptive technology because the cost of MOOCs to institutions does not meet Christensen's criteria. Furthermore, MOOCs' dominance, in terms of users, by people who already hold a degree suggests they may not be easy to use for the newcomer to higher education. In addition, a survey in the USA (Horrigan 2016) showed that 80% of the sample of 2752 did not have much awareness of MOOCs (p. 8) while, in the UK, the Universities and Colleges Information Systems Association (2014) argue that MOOCs have made little impression (p. 10) and are, 'a long way from being a mainstream concern' (p. 35). Christensen and Horn (2013) argue that MOOCs' early impact bore the hallmarks of a disruptive innovation, but MOOCs' dropout rates and the prior educational attainments of their successful completers indicate that MOOCs are not providing enough evidence to suggest they are creating new markets, or comprising low-end disruption either by drawing students away from traditional university education. MOOCs offer certificates for completion, the market value of which has yet to be demonstrated.

An alternative to MOOC certificates with potential market value is to have assessment on MOOCs which, itself, produces use value; this is an area of potential for MOOCs identified by Laurillard (2016) and thus MOOCs may find a niche in Continuing Professional Development (CPD), in which the outcome of the learning adds value to existing professional practice. The openness of MOOCs is thus limited to an organizational context (and MOOCs are no longer massive if they are limited to providing CPD within the confines of an organization), but the use value and educational potential of the MOOC can be enhanced by sharpening the definition of the MOOC's object, giving it a specific purpose. Viewed as an activity system, the clear identification of an object orientates the subject and focuses the use of the technology tool. However, removing the openness and the massiveness from MOOCs reinvents them as online courses, which have been around since the 1990s (Lawton and Katsomitros 2012), thus highlighting the argument that MOOCs are not truly innovative. That said, and despite curtailing the massiveness and openness of MOOCs, such decisive steps may be necessary in order for MOOCs to secure an effective, marketable and sustainable niche (Flavin 2016b).

The criticism of MOOCs may also be applied to Second Life, a virtual world peopled by participants' online personae, known as avatars, and launched in 2003. Second Life attracted encouraging comments about its value to higher education; Salmon (2009) argued, 'I believe that it [Second Life] and its successors are here to stay as significant players in the higher education field' (p. 535). Second Life was innovative, yet, and despite widespread publicity, it did not gain a substantial foothold in higher education because, in practice, it was not used extensively and was unable to build a sustainable niche (Livingstone 2011); an Organization for Economic Co-operation and Development study of students in the USA (2009, p. 15) found that less than 9% used Second Life or other virtual worlds. Furthermore, a meta-study of articles on Second Life covering the period 2005–2011 (Wang and Burton 2012) found that articles on Second Life rose in number from 2005 but declined from 2009, suggesting diminishing interest in the platform as a means of supporting learning and teaching.

Second Life has a relatively steep learning curve (the participant has to learn to move, interact, shift from one location to another, manage their online identity), and therefore does not conform to Christensen's core criteria. Carr (2009) writes of the 'relative emptiness' of Second Life, and that it is 'potentially confusing.' When new technologies for learning and teaching do not comply with Christensen's core criteria, they tend to fail, not least because learning to use a new technology can comprise a knowledge barrier, which users avoid by opting for easy to use technologies instead. Moore (2004) had linked Disruptive Innovation and fads, but there is a clear distinction between the two, centring on sustainability. This is a key reason why Disruptive Innovation is a process traceable over time, rather than a single event.

YouTube

Disruptive technologies get used by universities. Many universities have their own YouTube channels, as do individual departments. YouTube videos are available on subjects ranging across the entire higher education curriculum. YouTube videos also allow university branding within the YouTube brand, supplying educational content from a popular platform; explicitly education channels such as YouTube EDU and YouTube Teachers are available, simply and conveniently.

YouTube channels can be used to market a university as well as for learning and teaching, but the branding of YouTube adds complexity to the issue. Kim (2012) describes YouTube as an 'ad-friendly environment' (pp. 54, 56); students and lectures are exposed to commercial as well as educational content. Sanders (2011) notes, in relation to the economics of technology enhanced learning, 'the costs can only be recovered by the providers if there is the economy of scale found in a mass market, or when they are extensively subsidised through grants or advertising' (p. 66), but giving advertisers privileged access to students and lecturers raises ethical problems, and thus YouTube is not a problem-free platform for universities. It is disruptive because it is free, simple and convenient, but it is also a commercial, not philanthropic, platform. A disruption of communication channels is one thing, but a disruption of academic independence and responsibility is another, as is the dilution of a university's brand through the use of a commercial, third party (Flavin 2016b).

YouTube is a disruptive technology and it is also, like Google and Wikipedia, a hub technology, from which a range of resources can be accessed. Furthermore, the popularity of YouTube means it is familiar to many students and lecturers, who can navigate their way easily through it. That said, YouTube can also be thought of as an Efficiency Innovation, because it provides reusable content, with the lecturer's time and the university's resources only being used once, in the recording. If we combine

YouTube as an efficiency innovation with YouTube as a commercial platform giving advertisers access to students, we enter a potentially dystopian scenario in which academic jobs are threatened by being repositioned within the gig economy, and in which learning and teaching is suborned to commercial practices. Innovation does not have to be benign.

YouTube is a free, simple and convenient technology, but it is necessary to analyse patterns of consumption on YouTube in order to use the platform effectively for learning and teaching; Buzzetto-More (2014) showed, via a survey of 221 users, how the length of a YouTube video was a determinant in whether it was viewed, with shorter videos being preferred (pp. 28–29). Practice in relation to YouTube can eventually give rise to a distinctive pedagogy.

From a second generation Activity Theory perspective, the use of YouTube to support learning and teaching can impact on the division of labour, with resources outside the institution being accessed by students, and it can also have a wider impact on the community if a preference for short videos influences expectations of learning and teaching more widely. The lecture, the dominant pedagogical tool, is many things but it is rarely short. It is almost certainly the human interaction of the lecture that makes its length effective. YouTube videos and other videos benefit from brevity in the absence of physical co-presence, but brevity may inevitably limit depth of coverage. It is possible to create a sequence of brief videos to cover a topic in more depth, but doing so places a production burden on the content provider. YouTube is a disruptive technology but currently lacks a distinctive pedagogy to direct its usage in higher education.

THE PREDICTIVE VALUE OF DISRUPTIVE INNOVATION

Christensen and Raynor (2003) are explicit about the predictive value of Disruptive Innovation (p. 55). Christensen has, in fact, consistently asserted the predictive value of his theory: 'any assertion that the model has not or cannot be used to predict outcomes simply does not square with historical fact' (2006, p. 46).

The likely success or otherwise of a technology can be estimated by its conformity to Christensen's core criteria for disruptive technologies. However, the predictive capability of Disruptive Innovation has been challenged by Danneels (2006) and Lepore (2014), both of whom point to the failure of the Disruptive Growth Fund, with which Christensen was associated. The Fund, launched in 2000, gave financial support to disruptive innovations but closed within a year, having lost nearly two thirds of its value. That said, Danneels concedes that it may not have been a fair test of the theory, as the Fund was launched at the height of the tech bubble (pp. 2–3). Christensen (Bennett 2014) has downplayed his involvement with the Disruptive Growth Fund, but it remains a blemish on his theory.

Attempts have been made to develop and hone the predictive potential of Disruptive Innovation, for example, by Nagy et al. (2016), who present a three-step approach for defining and identifying disruptive technologies. Their definition of Disruptive Innovation is something 'that changes the performance metrics, or consumer expectations, of a market by providing radically new functionality, discontinuous technical standards, or new forms of ownership' (p. 4). The idea of ownership is especially relevant to this book; students and lecturers commonly carry around convenient and relatively low-cost technologies that have greater functionality and higher technical standards than the technologies supplied by their universities. Disruptive Innovation continues to be developed and its predictive value continues to be asserted as means of identifying disruptive technologies get refined.

This book has not sought to evaluate the predictive value of Disruptive Innovation as a primary aim, but the book does argue that technologies conforming to Christensen's criteria have shown themselves to be popular in supporting learning and teaching, which has implications for the design of learning technologies. Put plainly, if technologies are simple, easy to use, convenient and free, they are more likely to get used. This book argues that Disruptive Innovation is not predictive explicitly, but Christensen's original formulation of disruptive technologies identifies criteria that have resulted in the successful adoption of technologies by users. Furthermore, the disruptive potential of learning analytics (a free, convenient and easy to use technology) is noteworthy, as analytics can evaluate students' progress through educational systems, creating the potential to enhance the evidence base and predictive potential of Disruptive Innovation, as the popularity of emerging technologies can be gauged even as they are used. By monitoring technology usage through data and learning analytics, universities can be receptive and responsive to the use of new and potentially disruptive technologies. Christensen's core criteria for a disruptive technology can be applied by strategy makers to existing and emerging technologies for learning and teaching in higher education and thus Christensen's criteria can have a potentially predictive value. Christensen's core criteria succeed often enough to merit being considered when universities make strategic decisions about technologies.

Christensen et al. (2015) propose Apple's iPhone as a good example of Disruptive Innovation, the disruptiveness of which emerged through practice: 'The product that Apple debuted in 2007 was a sustaining innovation in the smartphone market: It targeted the same customers coveted by incumbents, and its initial success is likely explained by product superiority. The iPhone's subsequent growth is better explained by disruption – not of other smartphones but of the laptop as the primary access point to the internet.' The product spawned a new form of practice with phones but not a new practice per se; existing social and cultural practices determined the nature and extent of the disruptive innovation, highlighting the argument that there are parameters and limits to Disruptive Innovation. The iPhone facilitated disruptive usage through its ease of use, encouraging experimentation on the part of users; Pisano (2015) argues, 'Apple consistently focuses its innovation on making its products easier to use than competitors' (p. 7). The iPhone and similar devices are portable and provide quick and easy to use access to the internet from any location, comprising a disruptive technology. Furthermore, the iPhone came from a company outside the mobile phone industry. As O'Reilly and Tushman (2016) note, Nokia (the then market leader) focused on their competitors, Erickson, Sony and Motorola, ignoring the Apple iPhone and Google Android (p. 222), the latter being disruptive because it created, 'an ecosystem of application development atop its platform' (Wessel 2016), resembling the hub technology approach of Google, as the core technology enables a range of actions. The disruption of the mobile phone industry by outsiders was unexpected, which is consistent with the argument of Christensen et al. (2008): 'disruptive innovation does not take root through a direct attack on the existing system. Instead, it must go around and underneath the system' (p. 225). However, Apple products are not always wholly innovative; Chena et al. (2016) show that Apple's iPad was preceded by tablet computers from both HP and Dell, but it was Apple who achieved market success (p. 563). The success of Apple products where similar, competitors' products failed implies that marketing and branding play a part in the success of disruptive technologies, in line with the analysis of Disruptive Innovation offered by Markides (2006).

THE LIMITS OF DISRUPTIVE INNOVATION

Disruptive Innovation has parameters. Disruption is not an unfettered process. Markides (2006) argues it is possible to create disruption consciously through marketing, citing Amazon and Swatch, neither of which set out by creating a new product or service (Amazon did not invent bookselling) but both of which changed the way the product or service is experienced by the consumer (p. 20). Danneels (2004) also uses Amazon to critique Disruptive Innovation, arguing that Amazon started in the mainstream market, contrary to the argument that disruptive technologies flourish when they appeal to a peripheral or new customer base, though Wessel (2016) argues that the emergence of disruptive technologies at the low end of a market is a by-product rather than a central aspect of Disruptive Innovation. However, while not all innovations that cause disruption need to conform to Christensen's model, his core definition remains useful for identifying factors that make a new technology more likely to succeed within established markets and, more specifically (this book argues), within higher education.

This book accepts the modifications of Disruptive Innovation set down by Markides but goes further by incorporating Activity Theory and thus arguing that the limits of disruptive usage are also determined by broader factors, including history and economics. In addition, this book acknowledges the relevance of the revised definition of Disruptive Innovation offered by Nagy et al. (2016), comprising functionality, technical standards and ownership, with an emphasis, in this book, of the impact of ownership, through BYOD. The ease of use of BYOD, together with the functionality and technical standards of personally owned devices, comprises a significant disruptive innovation in higher education, significant not least because it is indicative of the increasing privatization of higher education. Universities claim to encourage collaborative learning, but both prices and practices are increasingly an individual concern. If we incorporate Nagy et al.'s (2016) definition of Disruptive Innovation, especially as it relates to ownership, we can identify Disruptive Innovation sooner, and form a sense of a new technology's potential and limitations from its early usage.

Viewed from an Activity Theory perspective, subjects (users) do not approach tools (technologies) as a limitless index of possibilities. Disruption is not the unfettered expression of creativity but is, instead, shaped by economic and social forces, which both offer and circumscribe possibilities for usage and which, in addition, are in states of flux themselves. Therefore, the shift from one activity system to another, caused by the accumulation of contradictions within an existing activity system, represents a significant change in possibility; new uses for a technology become possible within a new activity system, or, alternatively, new practices with technologies prompt the creation of new activity systems. Consequently, the use of disruptive technologies may signify a pressure towards the creation of a new activity system in higher education, in which the use of disruptive technologies to support learning and teaching is accepted and accommodated. This involves the acceptance of alternative pathways to knowledge and will have implications for assessment. Ultimately, Intended Learning Outcomes for modules and programmes may need to reflect the likelihood of a wider range of learning experiences to achieve specific objects, and objects themselves may need to be more flexible, acknowledging diverse pathways leading to the construction of new knowledge.

Limitations to Disruptive Innovation are generated by a range of factors, and therefore innovation is a structured, if not consciously managed, process. Innovation can be managed according to Markides (2006), but innovation emerges more fundamentally through practice; purpose is constructed rather than being decreed a priori through design. This book therefore argues for a range of responses to Disruptive Innovation, including the production of technology enhanced learning strategies based on practice rather than on the technologies themselves, recognizing that technologies have no inviolable, intrinsic purpose, but acquire purpose through human agency, realizing and releasing their disruptive potential through practice.

Some technologies function as hubs; students and lecturers go to Google, for example, before other resources, to access a range of materials to support learning and teaching (Flavin 2012, 2015, 2016a). As for why students and lecturers go to Google in preference to other sources, the market dominance of Google is clearly one factor. However, Markides (2006) is also useful for understanding user preferences, because Markides identifies the importance of marketing in relation to disruption and how marketing can prompt disruption, thus potentially destabilizing Christensen and Raynor's (2003) core contention that disruption emerges through practice, though it needs to be recognized that Markides was not writing about Google, but about disruption, as defined by Christensen, as a broader practice. The problem can be addressed by recognizing that disruption has parameters of possibility. Students and lecturers, within a second generation activity system, are themselves shaped by history, economics and culture, as well as by their individual life circumstances which are, in turn, shaped, right down to the fundamentals of consciousness itself, as argued by Vygotsky (1930) and Leontiev (1978). Therefore, the contexts experienced by students and lecturers have a deterministic effect on what they do with technologies, but new practices, however prompted, have the potential to change contexts because of the dynamic interaction between practices and contexts. Marketing influences technology usage, but it is only one of a range of factors influencing practice. Moreover, contradictions emerge; historically inherited and ingrained practices, such as accessing higher education learning materials through academic libraries, can be contradicted by technologies enabling simpler, easier and more convenient access to learning; Engeström et al. (2013) recognize, 'the digitization of information and the emergence of powerful web based tools of information storing and searching have led to a radical decrease in researchers' physical visits to library [sic] and also in their use of physical books and journals' (p. 88). The use of different tools can change the subject's perception of the object (the physical campus can become less important, thus affecting the community node of an activity system), and the subject's relationship with the division of labour can also change. Disruption is prompted and structured rather than the unfettered expression of human creativity. Technologies that are simple, convenient, cheap (or free) and easy to use are most likely to be used, and technologies are used in arterial and effective ways to accomplish specific tasks.

Disruptive Technology Enhanced Learning

Technologies are universal in supporting learning and teaching in higher education. Therefore, there is a need to use technology tools to their best effect in order to enhance learning and teaching and in order not to squander their learning and teaching possibilities.

At present, institutional technologies are underused relative to the use of disruptive technologies. A strategic approach based on known aspects of practice is more likely to be successful than an approach which starts with the technologies themselves: a report from the Technology Enhanced Learning Research Programme (Noss 2013) which poses the question in its introduction, 'how can we design technology that enhances learning...?' is surely asking the wrong question. It is better, this book argues, to start from practice.

Christensen's work is central to this book by providing a core definition of disruptive technologies (Christensen 1997, p. xv) and through the argument that disruption is about practice rather than design (Christensen and Raynor 2003). Activity Theory is also important to this book, especially because Engeström's (1987) second generation activity system enables an analysis of the impact of disruptive technologies on social relations in higher education. Moreover, Activity Theory, underpinned by the work of Vygotsky and others, challenges the notion of individual identity and argues that identity is formed by its contexts, including the social and the historical. The argument has implications for this book, which therefore eschews models of technology adoption focused on the individual. Instead, this book views practice as necessarily social; a range of factors contribute to and limit disruptive innovation and hence disruptive innovation is not rooted in the special talents of creative individuals. The process of innovation is observable, but it is apparent in social relations rather than individual psychology.

The Community of Practice theory (Lave and Wenger 1991; Wenger 1998) is used in this book to evaluate the extent to which the use of disruptive technologies determines progress and identity formation in a university community of practice. The Community of Practice theory also highlights how disruptive technologies can be perceived as threatening because of the challenge disruptive technologies pose to the shared repertoire of the community. By viewing universities as communities of practice, this book identifies technologies as aspects of identity construction, and disruptive technologies can disrupt but also enhance established communities. Disruptive technologies are a threat to the established norms of communities, though they can also assist communities if communities work with disruptive technologies. This book's distinctiveness is rooted in the fact that it adds Activity Theory and the Community of Practice to Disruptive Innovation, thus emphasizing practice, the wider social influences on practice and the impact of disruptive technologies on higher education communities over time.

It is possible to represent this book's core position through a figure.

Fig. 5.1 represents Disruptive Technology Enhanced Learning as a modified second generation activity system. Disruptive technologies are the tools used to produce successful learning and teaching experiences and outcomes. The use of disruptive technologies changes the division of labour and changes the relationship between the subject and the university. The community of the university is illuminated by the Community of Practice

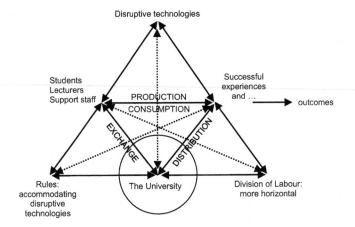

Fig. 5.1 Disruptive technology enhanced learning as a second generation activity system

theory, which acknowledges the role of the newcomer, who can be an important carrier and producer of innovation, networking with other subjects. Developing this representation, the most likely locus of contradiction evident in the figure is weighted towards the left hand side of the triangle, because community members using disruptive technologies and networking with other users create the conditions in which the community might have to reconsider its rules, recognizing the practices of lecturers and students, which contradict engrained practices such as the use of university libraries and module and programme reading lists. This is the area of higher education practice in which expansive learning is most likely to emerge, as the use of tools mounts a challenge to the rules of the community.

The disruptive use of technologies has implications for assessment in higher education in instances when students are accessing materials for learning via disruptive technologies rather than using reading lists supplied by lecturers. If the student is demonstrating attainment of the learning outcomes, then it is appropriate to credit the learning undertaken, but if the learning is undertaken by non-institutional pathways, it may pose a challenge for the university. In second generation Activity Theory terms, a contradiction may emerge between the technology node and the rules node, and academic judgements will need to be made in order to address the contradiction. Academic judgement may entail the disregard or relegation of learning undertaken non-institutionally, but a more imaginative approach would be to recognize and encourage the broader channels for learning made available through technology, encouraging and stewarding different pathways, not all of them institutional, for the construction of knowledge. There is a potential for disruptive technologies to enable and evidence more self-directed learning and more autonomy, qualities that universities aim to develop in their students.

If the university as an institution is willing to work with new practices, it may have to be willing to rethink its forms of assessment and its assessment criteria. The use of BYOD creates the conditions in which subjects can have successful experiences and outcomes with less explicit mediation through their university, while the use of learning analytics empowers the university to personalize subjects' learning pathways, modifying the existing curriculum but making successful learning experiences and outcomes more likely. That said, there is a potential conflict between BYOD and learning analytics, if the use of BYOD evades the detection systems of learning analytics, thus weakening the validity of the data that learning analytics generates.

The use of disruptive technologies has implications for the division of labour in higher education; students can access materials to support their learning by means other than through their university. More provocatively, if the free access to learning materials made available through disruptive technologies poses a threat to the high-fees offering of universities, entirely online colleges with minimal institutional library facilities could pose a threat to established providers (Flavin 2016b). Furthermore, and as an aspect of the transfer of the cost of higher education from the state to the individual, and hence the privatization of higher education, knowledge may become something purchased rather than freely available; while it is impossible to imagine the whole of knowledge being corralled in this way, academic journals might conceivably start charging individuals for access, as a supplement to institutional subscription.

The use of disruptive technologies has significant implications for universities. Christensen et al. (2006) describe catalytic innovations, which provide 'good-enough' solutions. They further argue, 'in the absence of alternatives, online courses remain an adequate option for an underserved population.' This is another possible market for the MOOC, providing higher education for those to whom the campus university is undesirable, unattainable or impractical, but the key test is the market value of the qualification, and higher education has been remarkably consistent in that regard, and with very little movement in universities' reputations over time.

The traditional degree of three or four years' duration continues to prevail over the alternative possibilities.

Established practices relating to module reading lists and academic libraries can be circumvented by users, who by-pass established, institutional technologies and manage their learning through simple, convenient and easy to use pathways, but the original prompt to learn formally and the broad direction of that learning comes, still, from the university. More widely, universities' best defence is that students continue to perceive them as vital, and the imprimatur of a university legitimizes, both explicitly and symbolically, students' achievements (Flavin 2016b). Christensen and Eyring (2011) argue, 'Universities have grown larger, more complex, and more expensive, but their basic character still reflects decisions made in the late nineteenth and early twentieth centuries' (p. 379), and Christensen et al. (2016) argue, 'Business models by their very nature are designed not to change, and they become less flexible and more resistant to change as they develop over time.' Contrary to Christensen et al. (2011), the business model of many traditional colleges and universities is not broken, but the business model persists in spite of actual practice, not because of it. The university as an institution, and individual universities as brands, will endure, but universities' strategies and claims for technology enhanced learning do not conflate with students' and lecturers' practices. The practice of students and lecturers embraces disruptive technologies, while the institutional rhetoric clings to the conservatism of Sustaining Innovation. The core university model is resilient and entrenched but it is not unassailable. The development of learning and teaching in universities is typified by the Sustaining Innovation approach, but pedagogies are produced in particular social circumstances (Daniels 2014, p. 21) and the internet in higher education, while now established and embedded, continues to have the potential to produce, or respond swiftly to, disruptive circumstances.

Universities should recognize that disruptive technology use happens; students and lecturers are more likely to use Google than an academic journal aggregator. Universities can choose to ignore the disruptive use of technologies but, in so doing, they will continue to produce technology enhanced learning strategies on an institutional level which are not aligned with the actual practices of students and lecturers. Furthermore, if universities ignore the disruptive use of technologies, they will continue to invest in underused institutional technologies.

UK University Technology Enhanced Learning Strategies

The publication of strategies for learning, teaching and assessment in higher education is practically ubiquitous: the Higher Education Funding Council for England (2009) acknowledged their importance in relation to technology enhanced learning (p. 2). Some universities also publish stand-alone technology enhanced learning strategies. In view of the prevalence of strategy documents, a small-scale research project was undertaken in summer 2016 to examine the extent to which Disruptive Innovation features in strategies for technology enhanced learning (Flavin and Quintero under review), a project which was useful for seeing the extent to which disruptive technologies and Disruptive Innovation are accommodated in higher education in the UK.

Forty-four UK university strategy documents were sampled. Of these, 10 were stand-alone technology enhanced learning strategies, while 34 were teaching and learning strategies with a technology enhanced learning component therein. The research project was specifically interested in the extent to which innovation features in strategies for technology enhanced learning, and in the balance in the strategies between practice on the one hand and technologies on the other, aiming to illuminate the extent to which Disruptive Innovation is an institutional concern or priority.

Of the 44 strategies sampled, 14 did not mention innovation at all. Twenty-four strategies mentioned innovation one to five times, and six strategies mentioned innovation 6–10 times. Two mentioned innovation nine times and two mentioned it 10 times (the most times it was mentioned); the average number of mentions for innovation was 2.8, with a mode of two.

Following an initial scan to note the uses of the specific term, 'innovation,' the 44 strategies were each read through in more detail and were coded in order to gain a qualitative sense of whether technology or practice with technologies was dominant. Specific practices were identified, including Disruptive Innovation and Sustaining Innovation, as were specific technologies, including Google. A five-point Likert scale was used to evaluate each strategy, with the following categories: 'technology very dominant,' 'technology quite dominant,' 'neither,' 'practice quite dominant' and 'practice very dominant.' The strategies were also read to evaluate whether they were stressing technologies or whether they were emphasizing practice, in the sense of what technologies enabled students and lecturers to do.

The results showed that technology was quite dominant in nine strategies, practice was quite dominant in 11 strategies, and practice was very dominant in six strategies. There were 18 strategies in which neither technologies nor practice were dominant. There were no strategies in which.

The results are shown in bar graph form below (Fig. 5.2).

In many cases, technology and practice were balanced in strategy documents, though with a slight weighting towards practice overall in the sample.

The term 'innovation' was counted in each strategy but, within the individual documents, the term was not always used in the sense intended by Christensen. There were instances in which innovation was linked, albeit implicitly, to disruption, but innovation was also commonly used as a synonym for change. The University of Edinburgh's 'IS Technology Enhanced Learning Strategy 2014–2017,' states, as part of its mission, 'We lead, innovate and collaborate to develop and support high quality learning technology that enriches student experience and outcomes' (University of Edinburgh 2014), a commitment which does not mention disruption. Innovation features in this strategy and others but practice is not preeminent. Instead, the technology cart leads the practice horse: a number of the strategies focused on how technologies enhance experience, but not

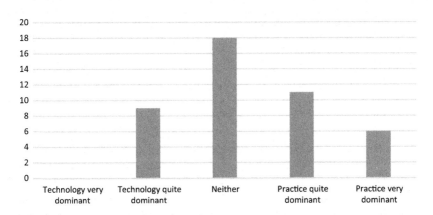

Fig. 5.2   The balance between practice and technologies in strategy documents, in relation to technology enhanced learning

about how practice determines which technologies are used, and not on the extent to which they are used innovatively.

The results suggest UK higher education institutions are adopting a Sustaining Innovation approach to technology enhanced learning as far as their strategies are concerned. Universities in the sample tend to prioritize practice over technology to a modest extent but are less keen to stress innovation, especially disruptive innovation. There is some evidence of innovation in technology enhanced learning, but it is along established and sustaining rather than disruptive lines. Innovation in technology enhanced learning in UK universities' strategy documents is commonly about making existing technologies serve learning and teaching more effi- ciently: 'make best use of technology to enhance provision' (University of Cambridge 2015, p. 2), or, 'IT services run effectively and efficiently, continually improving and enhancing to make our services reliable, available on demand and flexible enough to facilitate growth and adapt to change' (University of Cardiff 2013, p. 3).

The strategies suggest universities acknowledge the importance of prac- tice, but universities are seemingly less welcoming of innovation, especially disruptive innovation, a specific term which did not feature in any of the strategy documents sampled. That said, Queen Mary University's strategy acknowledged, implicitly, disruptive, sustaining and efficiency innovation: 'To use learning technologies to achieve efficiency (improving existing processes through cost, time benefits and scale), enhancement (improving existing learning opportunities) and transformation (new learning opportu- nities and processes) in order to improve the student experience' (Queen Mary University 2010). Furthermore, University College London's strat- egy, under a wider initiative of the Connected Curriculum, states, 'The Connected Curriculum... resonates fully with the principles of innovation and disruptive thinking that we associate with UCL's founders' (University College London 2016, p. 7). There were therefore isolated examples of Disruptive Innovation, if only by implication, but it was more commonplace to find commitments to Sustaining Innovation, applicable to both students and lecturers: 'To provide a learner-centred approach focusing on enhanc- ing the learner experience through the appropriate and consistent use of technology' (University of Sheffield 2012–2016, p. 2), or, 'We will develop appropriate online and other support materials for teaching and learning that will be readily available to all academic staff' (University College Birmingham 2015).

The examination of UK universities' technology enhanced learning strategies indicates a willingness to adapt on the part of universities but a disinclination to disrupt. Moreover, widespread practices by students, such as the use of Google, are largely ignored. The University of Exeter's (2009, rev. 2011) strategy does propose piloting 'the use of Google apps as a tool to support collaborative working' (p. 10), and the University of Greenwich (2013) mentions the use of Google Scholar (p. 7) and Google Docs (p. 9), but the focus in the strategies sampled is, consistently, on institutional technologies, which tend to be sustaining technologies.

As documents representing a university's commitment, if not necessarily its practice, strategies for technology enhanced learning signify institutional commitments to Sustaining Innovation; King and Boyatt (2014) argue that technology enhanced learning strategies 'offer visionary profiles for organizations and are not usually developed in consultation with staff; this can create tension in the workplace' (p. 1273), implying that a ground up approach is not used to inform strategies. Students' and lecturers' practice with disruptive technologies is largely ignored, despite being a key determinant of the purposes to which technologies are applied. Jones (2012) argues, 'the future of university provision is a choice and not the result of a technologically determined process' (p. 36) but, on the basis of the strategy documents sampled, the choices made are unimaginative, focused on making existing practice more efficient rather than rethinking practice.

CONCLUDING REMARKS

Despite the conservatism of the technology enhanced learning strategies researched for this book, there is no reason why universities cannot be more innovative in their approach to disruptive technologies and Disruptive Innovation. Universities have the means to encourage and support disruptive technologies.

Christensen et al. (2011) argue for Disruptive Innovation on an institutional level. Developing the possibilities of Disruptive Technology Enhanced Learning, universities can revisit module and programme aims and intended learning outcomes to recognize, via approaches to assessment, that students and lecturers have sources they use in preference to reading lists. Students and lecturers can be encouraged to use disruptive technologies to access new resources, thereby exhibiting autonomy and self-direction and enhancing learning and teaching for future cohorts. Lecturers and students might also, through technologies, design innovative and

effective assessment in preference to the essay and the exam, both of which are long established but tend in practice to encourage only limited use of what are, by now, established technologies. A technology such as the blog, for example, is conducive to the evidencing of reflection through its dated and timed entries, and is thus potentially well suited to academic assessment.

The challenge to universities is to understand and manage disruptive technologies, not just to safeguard academic standards but also to identify the disruptive use of technologies as an opportunity to enhance learning and teaching. This latter and bolder step involves recognizing the potential of Disruptive Technology Enhanced Learning, seeing it not as something to be contained but as something to work with in partnership with students and lecturers for the betterment of learning and teaching (Flavin 2016b). Disruptive technologies can be enabled by individuals and by networks but intervention is required to enable disruptive technologies on an institutional level. One way to do this is through institutional technology enhanced learning strategies that recognize and accommodate the use of disruptive technologies to support learning and teaching, mapping the means to use disruptive technologies to enhance learning and teaching. Students and lecturers should be supported in their uses of disruptive technologies.

The following are therefore offered as condensed, key points:

- Technologies conforming to Christensen's core criteria for disruption (1997, p. xv) are used widely to support learning and teaching.
- Institutional, designed for learning technologies such as VLEs are sustaining technologies, offering improvements in terms of convenience but without fundamentally changing learning and teaching.
- Students and lecturers demarcate their technology usage.
- The use of disruptive technologies to support learning and teaching in higher education has implications for assessment, for the division of labour in higher education and for the gatekeeper role of the university.
- Universities can engage constructively with disruptive technologies by recognizing that disruptive technologies are used widely by students and lecturers, and by rethinking technology enhanced learning strategies to accommodate Disruptive Technology Enhanced Learning.

The following, specific recommendations are offered:

- The production of technology enhanced learning strategies based on practice rather than on technologies, engaging with Disruptive Technology Enhanced Learning.
- The rethinking of institutional technologies, to see if they can be reconfigured in order to have the qualities outlined in Christensen's core definition of disruptive technologies.
- The welcoming of innovative practice by students and lecturers, accommodating innovation within, rather than excluding it from, learning and teaching, adopting an open borders approach to Disruptive Technology Enhanced Learning.
- The recognition that BYOD is becoming the norm.
- The use of learning analytics to create more personalized learning and to enhance student support.

In my own thinking, I started out with Christensen's dualism between sustaining and disruptive technologies. I took the view that VLEs were sustaining technologies, relocating the component parts of face-to-face teaching online but without due consideration of the deterministic effect of the medium. I also assumed that disruptive technologies were the most interesting, as they draw upon human creativity to create new possibilities for learning and teaching. In addition to Christensen's work, I was interested in Huizinga's (1971/1938) argument that play is a feature of human nature, something human beings do instinctively, and that play turns to seriousness, and hence simply experimenting with new technologies can lead over time to their adoption into formal practice. I also accepted the Community of Practice argument that learning is simply something human beings do.

However, I now take the more nuanced view that possibilities for disruption are structured and circumscribed; meaning is constructed from the prevailing economic and historical conditions, creating epistemological limits and limits of practice. This argument is underlined by Vygotsky (1930) and Leontiev (1977) in their view of how consciousness itself is constructed. Each activity system, under the pressure of its own internal contradictions, creates possibilities for disruption, but once those disruptions threaten the activity system, they will either be suppressed, or understood without the need for further action (Benson and Whitworth 2007), or a new activity system will emerge in which the disruptive form of practice is accommodated. That activity system will, in turn, produce its own inner contradictions leading, again, to new forms of practice in an unending dialectic. Put another way, and building from the arguments of Vygotsky (1930) and Leontiev (1977) through to Christensen's work, there is a palimpsest or collage quality to human subjects, and practice brings forth aspects of historically shaped creativity and thus repositions consciousness. When a network of innovative users is formed, it can cause disruptions and then institutions respond to disruption, either through exclusion or with accommodation. To date, the established university model has been resilient in the face of change, but the internet has changed practice on a number of levels and it is presumptuous to continue to rely on the imperviousness of the university and its established learning and teaching model. Disruptive Technology Enhanced Learning is already rife in universities.

We do not engage constructively with disruptive technologies. Instead, we invest in costly and underused institutional systems. We can be confident that students and lecturers make plentiful use of disruptive technologies but we do not build that knowledge into strategies. We posit a hypothetical student who discusses issues on VLE forums and does his/her research via an academic journal aggregator, but actual learners are more likely to use VLEs as content repositories than as platforms for learning and teaching, while they undertake their research on Google and Wikipedia. As Lawrence (2015) argues, 'today's students are rejecting previously-held beliefs about how to conduct research and forging their own unique path towards scholarship' (p. 89). Most students and lecturers do not participate (they do not upload content to the internet, as shown in an Australian context by Corrin et al. (2010)), but students and lecturers do self-medicate, taking what they need from the wide range of sources available (Flavin 2016b). Hargittai and Walejko (2008) put forward a similar argument but refer to 'mere consumers of material' (p. 240). However, consumption is not an inferior form of practice, but is the outcome of students and lecturers getting jobs done by simple and convenient means.

The future of technology enhanced learning in higher education is not virtual worlds. The future is not the MOOC, which has limited impact, though the MOOC may transpire to have value as a means of marketing a university and its expertise, and may also find a learning and teaching market in Continuing Professional Development, compromising its massiveness and openness to achieve a specific goal, and compromising its innovative aspects too, as it becomes another version of an online course. The future is foretold in current practice and shows that simple, convenient and easy to use technologies support learning and teaching in higher education. If universities want their students and lecturers to use institutional technologies they would be well advised to design technologies in line with these criteria but also to allow practice to determine a purpose quite distinct from designers' intentions. Salmon et al. (2015) argue, in relation to online course design, 'more is not always better. Instead, more options may lead to confusion, intimidation, and learners who log off altogether' (p. 11) and an interviewee in my own research stated, 'Adding too many technologies to support teaching/learning, especially where one or two can do the job well, can overwhelm the student (and the educator!)' (Flavin 2012). This book therefore recommends making technologies simple and convenient and further recommends observing what students and lecturers do with technologies and the purposes they create for them.

It is, moreover, appropriate to recognize that Disruptive Innovation occurs within institutional and sectoral contexts. Observing practice and context will enable pattern recognition (Mukunda 2010); learning analytics can be used not to control and contain, but to support and to diversify the curriculum and the learning and teaching experience. BYOD is the most obvious disruptive technology in higher education at present, which carries the risk, for institutions, of increasingly underused institutional systems and thus technological redundancy. If universities' technology systems are, in practice, content repositories and no more, this should prompt a rethink of universities' investments in technologies, focused on having the necessary, high-quality infrastructure to support BYOD.

If we look at what students and lecturers do, rather than what we would like them to do, we will have a firmer evidence base from which to construct technology enhanced learning strategies and an enhanced knowledge of actual practices with technologies to support learning and teaching, thereby influencing the modules and programmes we design, the assessment methodologies we implement and the way we structure and support learning. Higher education will benefit from new activity systems in which the division of labour is reconsidered, to accommodate and support the presence of Disruptive Technology Enhanced Learning. We need more disruptive behaviour.

References

Amador, P., & Amador, J. (2014). Academic advising via Facebook: Examining student help seeking. *Internet and Higher Education, 21*, 9–16.

Bennett, D. (2014, June 21). Clayton Christensen responds to *New Yorker* takedown of "Disruptive Innovation". *Bloomberg Business*. Retrieved from http://

www.bloomberg.com/bw/articles/2014-06-20/clayton-christensen-responds-to-new-yorker-takedown-of-disruptive-innovation

Benson, A., & Whitworth, A. (2007). Technology at the planning table: Activity theory, negotiation and course management systems. *Journal of Organisational Transformation and Social Change, 4*(1), 75–92.

Bosch, T. E. (2009). Using online social networking for teaching and learning: Facebook use at the University of Cape Town. *Communicatio: South African Journal for Communication Theory and Research, 35*(2), 185–200.

Burd, E. L., Smith, S. P., & Reisman, S. (2015). Exploring business models for MOOCs in higher education. *Innovative Higher Education, 40,* 37–49.

Buzzetto-More, N. A. (2014). An examination of undergraduate student's perceptions and predilections of the use of You Tube in the teaching and learning process. *Interdisciplinary Journal of E-Learning and Learning Objects, 10,* 17–32.

Camus, M., Hurt, N. E., Larson, L. R., & Prevost, L. (2016). Facebook as an online teaching tool: Effects on student participation, learning, and overall course performance. *College Teaching, 64*(2), 84–94.

Carr, D. (2009). Learning and virtual worlds. In *Education 2.0? Designing the web for learning and teaching: A commentary by the technology enhanced learning phase of the teaching and learning research programme.* London: London Knowledge Lab, University of London.

Chena, C., Zhang, J., & Guoc, R.-S. (2016). The D-Day, V-Day, and bleak days of a disruptive technology: A new model for ex-ante evaluation of the timing of technology disruption. *European Journal of Operational Research, 251,* 562–574.

Christensen, C. M. (1997). *The innovator's dilemma: When new technologies cause great firms to fail.* Boston: Harvard Business School Press.

Christensen, C. M. (2006). The ongoing process of building a theory of disruption. *The Journal of Product Innovation Management, 23,* 39–55.

Christensen, C. M., & Eyring, H. J. (2011). *The innovative university: Changing the DNA of higher education from the inside out.* San Francisco: Jossey-Bass.

Christensen, C., & Horn, M. (2013, February 20). Beyond the buzz, where are MOOCs really going? *Wired opinion.* Retrieved from http://www.wired.com/2013/02/beyond-the-mooc-buzz-where-are-they-going-really/

Christensen, C. M., & Raynor, M. E. (2003). *The innovator's solution: Creating and sustaining successful growth.* Boston: Harvard Business School Press.

Christensen, C. M., Baumann, H., Ruggles, R., & Sadtler, T. M. (2006). Disruptive innovation for social change. *Harvard Business Review, 84*(12), 94–101.

Christensen, C. M., Horn, M. B., & Johnson, C. W. (2008). *Disrupting class: How disruptive innovation will change the way the world learns.* New York: McGraw-Hill.

Christensen, C.M., Horn, M.B., Caldera, L., & Soares, L. (2011). *Disrupting college: How disruptive innovation can deliver quality and affordability to postsecondary education*. Mountain View: Center for American Progress and Innosight Institute. Retrieved from https://cdn.americanprogress.org/wp-con tent/uploads/issues/2011/02/pdf/disrupting_college_execsumm.pdf

Christensen, C. M., Raynor, M. E., & McDonald, R. (2015). What is disruptive innovation? *Harvard Business Review, 93*(12), 44–53.

Christensen, C. M., Bartman, T., & van Bever, D. (2016, Fall). The hard truth about business model innovation. *MIT Sloan Management Review*. Retrieved from http://sloanreview.mit.edu/article/the-hard-truth-about-business-model-innovation/

Corrin, L., Bennett, S., & Lickyer, L. (2010). Digital natives: Everyday life versus academic study. In L. Dirckinck-Holmfeld, V. Hodgson, C. Jones, M. de Laat, D. McConnell, & T. Ryberg (Eds.), *Proceedings of the 7th international conference on networked learning*. Lancaster: Lancaster University.

Daniels, H. (2014). Vygotsky and dialogic pedagogy. *Cultural-Historical Psychology, 10*(3), 19–29.

Danneels, E. (2004). Disruptive technology reconsidered: A critique and research agenda. *The Journal of Product Information Management, 21*, 246–258.

Danneels, E. (2006). From the guest editor: Dialogue on the effects of disruptive technology on firms and industries. *The Journal of Product Information Management, 23*, 2–4.

Diver, P., & Martinez, I. (2015). MOOCs as a massive research laboratory: Opportunities and challenges. *Distance Education, 36*(1), 5–25.

Eijkman, H. (2010). Academics and Wikipedia: Reframing Web2.0+ as a disruptor of traditional academic power-knowledge arrangements. *Campus-Wide Information Systems, 27*(3), 173–185.

Ellison, N. B., Steinfield, C., & Lampe, C. (2011). Connection strategies: Social capital implications of Facebook-enabled communication practices. *New Media and Society, 20*(10), 1–20.

Engeström, Y. (1987). *Learning by expanding: An activity-theoretical approach to developmental research*. Helsinki: Orienta-Konsultit Oy. Retrieved from http://lchc.ucsd.edu/MCA/Paper/Engestrom/expanding/toc.htm

Engeström, Y. (1999). Innovative learning in work teams: Analyzing cycles of knowledge creation in practice. In Y. Engeström, R. Miettinen, & R. L. Punamaki (Eds.), *Perspectives on activity theory* (pp. 377–406). Cambridge: Cambridge University Press.

Engeström, Y., Rantavuori, J., & Kerosuo, H. (2013). Expansive learning in a library: Actions, cycles and deviations from instructional intentions. *Vocations and Learning, 6*, 81–106.

Fewkes, A. M., & McCabe, M. (2012). Facebook: Learning tool or distraction? *Journal of Digital Learning in Teacher Education, 28*(3), 92–98.

Flavin, M. (2012). Disruptive technologies in higher education. *Research in Learning Technology, 20*, 102–111.

Flavin, M. (2015). Home and away: The use of institutional and non-institutional technologies to support learning and teaching. *Interactive Learning Environments*. http://dx.doi.org/10.1080/10494820.2015.1041404

Flavin, M. (2016a). Disruptive conduct: The impact of disruptive technologies on social relations in higher education. *Innovations in Education and Teaching International, 15*(1), 3–15.

Flavin, M. (2016b). Technology-enhanced learning and higher education. *Oxford Review of Economic Policy, 32*(4), 632–645.

Flavin, M., & Quintero, V. (under review). UK Universities' technology enhanced learning strategies: A disruptive innovation perspective.

Gallagher, S., & Garrett, D. (2013). *Disruptive education: Technology-enabled universities*. The United States Study Centre, University of Sydney. Retrieved from http://apo.org.au/resource/disruptive-education-technology-enabled-universities

Gordon, N. (2014). *Flexible pedagogies: Technology-enhanced learning*. York: Higher Education Academy.

Hargittai, E., & Walejko, G. (2008). The participation divide: Content creation and sharing in the digital age. *Information, Communication and Society, 11*(2), 239–256.

Higher Education Funding Council for England. (2009). *Enhancing learning and teaching through the use of technology: A revised approach to HEFCE's strategy for e-learning*. Bristol: HEFCE.

Horrigan, J.B. (2016). *Lifelong learning and technology*. Pew Research Center. Retrieved from http://www.pewinternet.org/2016/03/22/lifelong-learning-and-technology/

Hrastinski, S., & Aghaee, N. M. (2012). How are campus students using social media to support their studies? An explorative interview study. *Education and Information Technologies, 17*, 451–464.

Huizinga, J. (1971, original work published 1938). *Homo Ludens*. Boston: Beacon Press.

Irwin, C., Ball, L., Desbrow, B., & Leveritt, M. (2012). Students' perceptions of using Facebook as an interactive learning resource at university. *Australasian Journal of Educational Technology, 28*(7), 1221–1232.

Johnson, L., Adams-Becker, S., Cummins, M., Estrada, V., Freeman, A., & Hall, C. (2016). *NMC horizon report: 2016 higher education edition*. Austin: The New Media Consortium.

Jones, C. (2012). Networked learning, stepping beyond the net generation and digital natives. In L. Dirckinck-Holmfeld, V. Hodgson, & D. Mc Connell (Eds.), *Exploring the theory, pedagogy and practice of networked learning* (pp. 27–41). New York: Springer.

Karlsson, N. (2014). The crossroads of academic electronic availability: How well does Google Scholar measure up against a university-based metadata system in 2014? *Current Science, 10*, 1661–1665.

Kim, J. (2012). The institutionalization of You Tube: From user-generated content to professionally generated content. *Media, Culture and Society, 34*(1), 53–67.

King, E., & Boyatt, R. (2014). Exploring factors that influence adoption of e-learning within higher education. *British Journal of Educational Technology, 46*(6), 1272–1280.

Laurillard, D. (2013). Foreword to the second edition. In H. Beetham & R. Sharpe (Eds.), *Rethinking pedagogy for a digital age* (2nd ed.). Abingdon: Routledge.

Laurillard, D. (2014). *What is the problem for which MOOCs are the solution?* #ALTC Blog: News and Views from the ALT community. Retrieved from https://altc.alt.ac.uk/blog/2014/06/what-is-the-problem-for-which-moocs-are-the-solution/

Laurillard, D. (2016). The educational problem that MOOCs could solve: Professional development for teachers of disadvantaged students. *Research in Learning Technology, 24.* http://www.researchinlearningtechnology.net/index.php/rlt/article/view/29369

Lave, J., & Wenger, E. (1991). *Situated learning: Legitimate peripheral participation.* Cambridge: Cambridge University Press.

Lawrence, K. (2015). Today's college students: Skimmers, scanners and efficiency-seekers. *Information Services and Use, 35*, 89–93.

Lawton, W., & Katsomitros, A. (2012). *MOOCs and disruptive innovation: The challenge to HE business models.* The Observatory on Borderless Higher Education. Retrieved from http://www.obhe.ac.uk/documents/view_details?id=929

Leontiev, A. N. (1977). Activity and consciousness. In *Philosophy of the USSR, problems of dialectical materialism* (trans. Daglish, R.). Moscow: Progress. Retrieved from https://www.marxists.org/archive/leontev/works/1977/leon1977.htm

Leontiev, A. N. (1978). *Activity, consciousness and personality* (trans. Hall, M.J.). Englewood Cliffs: Prentice Hall.

Lepore, J. (2014). The disruption machine: What the Gospel of innovation gets wrong. *The New Yorker, 90*(17), 30–36.

Livingstone, D. (2011). Second life is dead: Long live second life? *Educause Review, 46*(2), 61–62.

Liyanagunawardena, T. R., Lundqvist, K. O., & Williams, S. A. (2015). Who are with us: MOOC learners on a FutureLearn course. *British Journal of Educational Technology, 46*(3), 557–569.

Manca, S., & Ranieri, M. (2013). Is it a tool suitable for learning? A critical review of the literature on Facebook as a technology-enhanced learning environment. *Journal of Computer Assisted Learning, 29*(6), 487–504.

Manca, S., & Ranieri, M. (2016). Facebook and the others. Potentials and obstacles of social media for teaching in higher education. *Computers and Education, 95*, 216–230.

Markides, C. (2006). Disruptive innovation; in need of better theory. *The Journal of Product Innovation Management, 23*, 19–25.

Mazman, S. G., & Usluel, Y. K. (2010). Modeling educational usage of Facebook. *Computers and Education, 55*(2), 444–453.

Moore, G. (2004). Darwin and the demon. *Harvard Business Review, 82*(7–8), 86–92.

Mukunda, G. (2010). We cannot go on: Disruptive innovation and the First World War Royal Navy. *Security Studies, 19*, 124–159.

Nagy, D., Schussler, J., & Dubinsky, A. (2016). Defining and identifying disruptive innovations. *Industrial Marketing Management, 57*, 119–126.

Ng'ambi, D. (2015). Editorial: Massive open online courses (MOOCs): Disrupting teaching and learning practices in higher education. *British Journal of Educational Technology, 46*(3), 451–454.

Noss, R. (2013). *Does technology enhance learning? Some findings from the UK's technology enhanced learning research programme.* Retrieved from http://www.tlrp.org/docs/enhance.pdf

O'Reilly, C. A., & Tushman, M. L. (2016). *Lead and disrupt: How to solve the innovator's dilemma.* Stanford: Stanford Business Books.

Organisation for Economic Co-operation and Development, Centre for Educational Research and Innovation. (2009). *New millennium learners in higher education: Evidence and Policy Implications.* Paris: OECD, CERI.

Pisano, G. P. (2015). You need an innovation strategy. *Harvard Business Review, 93*(6), 3–12.

Queen Mary University. (2010). *Learning, teaching and assessment strategy.* London: Queen Mary University. Retrieved from http://www.qmul.ac.uk/docs/about/21996.pdf

Rowe, J. (2014). Student use of social media: When should the university intervene? *Journal of Higher Education Policy and Management, 36*(3), 241–256.

Salmon, G. (2009). The future for (second) life and learning. *British Journal of Educational Technology, 40*(3), 526–538.

Salmon, G., Ross, B., Pechenkina, E., & Chase, A. M. (2015). The space for social media in structured online learning. *Research in Learning Technology, 23*, 1–14.

Sanders, J. (2011). The challenge of cost-effective technology enhanced learning for medical education. *Education for Primary Care, 22*, 66–69.

Selwyn, N. (2009). Faceworking: Exploring students' education-related use of Facebook. *Learning, Media and Technology, 34*, 157–174.

Timmis, S. (2012). Constant companions: Instant messaging conversations as sustainable supportive study structures amongst undergraduate peers. *Computers and Education, 59*, 3–18.

Tower, M., Latimer, S., & Hewitt, J. (2014). Social networking as a learning tool: Nursing students' perception of efficacy. *Nurse Education Today, 34*(6), 1012–1017.

Universities and Colleges Information Systems Association. (2014). *2014 survey of technology enhanced learning for higher education in the UK.* Oxford: University of Oxford.

University College Birmingham. (2015). *Teaching, learning and assessment strategy 2015–2020.* Birmingham: University College Birmingham. Retrieved from http://applications.ucb.ac.uk/teaching-and-learning-assessment-strategy

University College London. (2016). *Education strategy 2016–21.* London: University College London. Retrieved from https://www.ucl.ac.uk/teaching-learning/2016-21/index/edit/UCL_Education_Strategy_Final_Web.pdf

University of Cambridge. (2015). *Learning and teaching strategy 2015–18.* Cambridge: University of Cambridge. Retrieved from http://www.educationalpolicy.admin.cam.ac.uk/files/lts_15-18.pdf

University of Cardiff. (2013). *University IT strategy 2013/14–2016/7.* Cardiff: University of Cardiff. Retrieved from http://www.cardiff.ac.uk/insrv/resources/UniversityITstrategy.pdf

University of Edinburgh. (2014). *IS technology enhanced learning strategy.* Edinburgh: University of Edinburgh. Retrieved from http://www.ed.ac.uk/files/imports/fileManager/IS%20Technology%20Enhanced%20Learning%20Strategy.pdf

University of Exeter. (2009, rev. 2011). *Technology enhanced learning strategy 2009–2015 (Revised September 2011).* Exeter: University of Exeter. Retrieved from https://as.exeter.ac.uk/media/level1/academicserviceswebsite/studentandstaffdevelopment/educationenhancement/pdfs/Attachment_B_-_TEL_strategy_2010_-_2015_Sept_2011_revision.pdf

University of Greenwich. (2013). *Finding new ways to teach, learn and discover: University of Greenwich Information and Technology Strategy 2013–2017.* Greenwich: University of Greenwich. Retrieved from http://www.gre.ac.uk/__data/assets/pdf_file/0011/907553/IT-Strategy-Final.pdf

University of Sheffield. (2012). *E-learning strategy at the University of Sheffield, 2012–2016.* Sheffield: University of Sheffield. Retrieved from https://www.sheffield.ac.uk/polopoly_fs/1.408155!/file/e-learningstrategy2012-16.pdf

Vygotsky, L. (1930). The socialist alteration of man. In R. Van Der Veet & J. Valsiner (Eds.), *The Vygotsky reader* (pp. 175–184). Oxford: Blackwell.

Wang, F., & Burton, J. K. (2012). Second life in education: A review of publications from its launch to 2011. *British Journal of Educational Technology, 44*(3), 357–371.

Wang, Q., Woo, H. L., Quek, C. L., Yang, Y., & Liu, M. (2012). Using the Facebook group as a learning management system: An exploratory study. *British Journal of Educational Technology, 43*(3), 428–438.

Wenger, E. (1998). *Communities of practice: Learning, meaning, and identity.* Cambridge: Cambridge University Press.

Wenger, E., White, N., & Smith, J. D. (2009). *Digital habitats: Stewarding technology for communities.* Portland: CPsquare.

Wessel, M. (2016). How big data is changing disruptive innovation. *Harvard Business Review.* Retrieved from https://hbr.org/2016/01/how-big-data-is-changing-disruptive-innovation

Yang, D., Wen, M., Howley, I., Kraut, R. and Rose, C. (2015). Exploring the effect of confusion in discussion forums of massive open online courses. *L@S 2015: Learning at Scale* (pp. 121–130). Vancouver.

Yuan, L. & Powell, S. (2013). *MOOCs and open education: Implications for higher education.* JISC and Cetis. Retrieved from http://publications.cetis.ac.uk/2013/667

INDEX

Note: Page numbers with "n" denote notes.

© The Author(s) 2017

M. Flavin, *Disruptive Technology Enhanced Learning*,
DOI 10.1057/978-1-137-57284-4